INCULTURATION

Intercultural and Interreligious Studies

edited by

ARIJ A. ROEST CROLLIUS, S.J.

XXI

CENTRE "CULTURES AND RELIGIONS" – PONTIFICAL GREGORIAN UNIVERSITY

INCULTURATED PASTORAL PLANNING

The U.S. Hispanic Experience

Michael Connors, C.S.C.
University of Notre Dame

ROME 2001

ISBN 88-7652-882-2

EDITRICE PONTIFICIA UNIVERSITÀ GREGORIANA

Piazza della Pilotta, 35 - 00187 Roma

CONTENTS

LIST OF DIAGRAMS

FOREWORD

More than ever before, the Church needs a true "praxis" theology, one that respects equally the intellectual and spiritual traditions of Christianity, while it "weaves," or contextualizes these traditions with the many concerns of the world. Not only must there be a praxis, however, but with it an increased sensitivity to the various cultures that give unique shape to the local churches. In his recent work, *Église d'églises: l'ecclesiologie de communion* (*Church of Churches: The Ecclesiology of Communion*), J.-M. R. Tillard wrote, relative to the Eucharist as our confession of faith,

> Such a confession has very profound implications: that is, the simple fact that Christian communities rooted in different cultures, representing different social contexts, linked to different expressions of faith, adopting different liturgies, mutually recognize their respective eucharists, constitutes a confession of the universality of salvation. [French ed., p. 261]

Tillard appreciates the difference between unity and uniformity in the building of *communio*, or *koinonia*, the Greek word carrying ancient philosophical connotations of life-giving participation. With the Trinity as the divine model of such participation, Christians, and in this case Catholics, should be able to grasp the significance of the union of diverse members.

Michael Connors has been sensitive to this urgency ever since his student days, carrying it over into his ongoing academic and pastoral activities. The present volume is the result of careful research and field work that shaped it in its dissertation form. Especially painstaking is Connors' research into the encuentros (encounters, planning sessions) leading up to the *National Pastoral Plan for Hispanic Ministry*. He has researched the literature on inculturation and employed it in his study of Hispanic Catholic (especially Mexican American Catholic) communities in the United States. Thus, the message of Vatican Council II and the history of events leading up to it receive careful attention in this work. Nor does Connors neglect the cultural anthropology dimensions of his research.

One finds in this book an example of how pastoral experience has been interfaced with interviews of Hispanic leaders in order to gauge the effectiveness of the *Pastoral Plan*. Further, this study is set in the light of the troubled history of relations between the United States and Mexico, and deals with the subtleties of the situation of "Mexican Americans." Connors is well aware that "Mexico" was once part of a huge area, including the state of California, called "New Spain." Hence his theological and pastoral project takes on the power of political analysis as well, enabling him to initiate some experimental thought not only on inculturation but on authentic liberation. It is to his greater credit that he listens to the voices of Mexicans and other Hispanics to testify to the importance of building a Church that deeply respects all local cultures. He has lent even greater weight to the well-known criteria for local theology developed by Robert Schreiter, enfleshing them within a community of people who will certainly be deeply influential in the future of North America as well as the universal Church.

Bernard Lonergan and his more recent commentator Frederick Crowe have called upon the Church to be a "learning Church" in order to honestly serve as a "teaching Church." Connors has presented us with a creative "case study" of how the Church might implement these ideas in its theology and pastoral practice. I enthusiastically welcome this volume and hope for many others of the same genre.

Carl F. Starkloff, S.J.
Institute of Jesuit Sources
Saint Louis University

Dedicated to the Hispanic people of the United States,
truly "a blessing from God."

"The relevance of this Council for the life both of the Church and the world can hardly be emphasized enough. Vatican II will be for the Church an all-embracing, paradoxical event of joy and distress, of hope and uncertainty, of spiritual richness and unthinkable humiliations."

Marcello de Carvalho Azevedo
Inculturation and the Challenges of Modernity

CHAPTER ONE

Culture as a Theological Locus

Faith and Context

Several years of full-time pastoral ministry in the U.S. left me both exhilarated and exhausted, inspired and yet perplexed. These were years of adjustment, celebration, fatigue, frustration, affirmation and much personal and professional growth. Parish work has many different facets. Demands of varying kinds, presented through people of diverse personalities, cultural backgrounds and religious stances, call upon the minister to develop a broad spectrum of practical skills. Indeed, it is difficult to imagine an occupation which makes more wide-ranging claims upon the wits and good will of the minister. Shrinking resources and the burgeoning expectations of parishioners in the post-Vatican II Roman Catholic Church only compound the matter.

My experience of working on the pastoral team of a parish formed in me the conviction that that ministry, in particular, suffers from a lack of adequate reflection upon its goals, relationships and strategies. That is to say, what transpires in a Roman Catholic parish frequently happens unreflectively. Repetition tends to count for more on the practical level than either discerning the pastoral needs of people in one's context, or a fresh confrontation with the classic sources of Christian tradition. The result, institutionally, is often that rigidity, staleness and narrowness which customarily accompany any "applied" theory-to-practice model.

At its best, on a day-to-day level, much of pastoral ministry involves listening and attending: counseling, collaborating with professional peers and volunteers, accompanying families in moments of joy and grief. Other moments invite the minister to diverse forms of speech: committee meetings, catechesis, preaching. For me personally, I was never more aware of the collision between the living word of Christian faith and the structures, concerns and stresses of people's daily lives than when I stepped into the pulpit. The crafting and delivery of a homily, week after week (almost day after day), taxed to the limit my abilities to remain accountable both to the tradition and to the real-life social situation of the people.

Over the years, parish ministry induced me to grow in awareness of the unwritten rules and the intangible resources operative in our social milieu. That is to say, I became more reflectively conscious of the culture of my people. I learned, for example, about the isolation and alienation of people in the highly individualistic environment of this society, and the concomitant hunger for authentic community. At the same time, I was forced to confront the paucity of cultural forms and supports for the cultivation of community life. It often seemed to me that all of us, ministers and ordinary folk alike, were caught up in forces of which we were only dimly aware. Those forces could at some times resonate powerfully with the Christian message. At other times, however, they could pose themselves as inimical to the very understanding of the message, or to the living out of the message, or both. In short, to be an American Catholic Christian at this historical moment is to be at cross-purposes with oneself, on several counts. Such matters invite an interminable amount of reflection, prayer, study – the time for which is all too rare in the busy schedule of pastoral ministry.

Our problem is not altogether new. Over the centuries, Christian faith has found itself confronted by, and embedded within, a wide variety of social milieux. Inevitably the church both shapes and is shaped by the cultural forces in which it lives. The founder of the Christian movement himself, Jesus of Nazareth, has to be understood within the Jewish culture of 1st-century Palestine. And within a short time of his death, the followers of Jesus faced a serious crisis as their Good News spread beyond Judaism and began to take up residence in the surrounding Gentile Hellenistic culture (cf. Acts 15). The nexus of faith and culture has remained a profound and controversial challenge through succeeding generations of Christianity.

In some respects, however, the theological problem of culture has grown even more acute in our time. The 19th and 20th centuries have some poignant lessons to teach us about culture's capacity to enlist religious sentiment in pursuit of unholy aims. Certainly one thinks of the grotesque evils of colonialism, fascism, apartheid, environmental despoliation, genocide and war. Moreover, global communications and transportation, together with a heightened consciousness of the ambiguities of both history and language, all have engendered a much greater sensitivity to the plurality of cultural realities which mark human life. But, if the times demand a more intentional and critical approach to the dynamic interaction of faith and culture, they also provide certain reflexive tools – the anthropological notion of *culture* itself is a peculiarly modern one – by which the church may hope to strive toward a still more "catholic" embrace of all peoples in its discovery and proclamation of the divine salvific will.

"A theology," wrote Bernard Lonergan, "mediates between a cultural matrix and the significance and role of a religion in that matrix."[1] The theologian always both speaks from within a culturally conditioned context, and to one or more such contexts, for there is no human life, and therefore no faith and no religion, which is not so conditioned. Thus, the paradigm for all theological endeavor can be summed up in David Tracy's felicitous word, "conversation." As Tracy says,

---

1. *Method in Theology* (Minneapolis: Seabury/Winston, 1972), p. xi.

"There is no intellectual, cultural, political, or religious tradition of interpretation that does not ultimately live by the quality of its conversation."[2] The mediating efforts we call theology are an essential praxis of the church, whose faith and tradition bear the impulse of mission to the world. That the world also influences the tradition is guaranteed by the church's indispensable utilization of language.

So the conversation continues, only today more self-consciously and critically. One evidence of the intensified interest in this dialogue is the introduction of a new crop of theological constructs. Two that are of central interest here are *inculturation*, and its cousin, *contextualization*. Despite the fact that both words are of relatively recent vintage, a considerable and still growing body of literature clusters around them. Both terms, of course, need to be clearly defined and understood if they are to lend any clarity to the faith-culture conversation. For the moment it is enough to note that, while the two are not quite synonymous, they both denote that the social context is to be taken seriously as a theological dialogue partner.

The present project is located within the horizon of the contemporary theology of inculturation. That concept and its attendant reflection serve as fundamental points of reference and analytic tools in the generation of the study's conclusions. The understanding of inculturation employed here is, in short, a balanced, dialogical one that attempts to respect and mediate the demands for both adaptation to a cultural setting and prophetic critique of that setting. This understanding thus envisions a range of possible stances toward and responses to particular cultures.

In two significant respects, however, this study edges to the frontiers of the theology of inculturation. In the first place, contemporary reflection on inculturation has been occasioned largely by the rapid growth of the church in the traditional societies of the so-called "Third World" of Asia, Africa and Latin America. In contrast, the project undertaken here focusses on a minority context within a "First World" nation, viz., the Hispanic community within the United States of America. Secondly, until quite recently the preponderance of the discussion of inculturation has tended to focus either on liturgical adaptation or on doctrinal catechesis. The purview of the present study is, rather, the whole of pastoral praxis. Here liturgy and formation are but two of a number of important concerns embraced within a comprehensive, unified perspective.

The Research Question

The relative novelty of this approach, as we shall see, is also inherent in the object under study. That object is a document known as the *National Pastoral Plan*

---

2. *Plurality and Ambiguity: Hermeneutics, Religion, Hope* (San Francisco: Harper & Row, 1987), p. ix.

for Hispanic Ministry.[3] As an official attempt to reflect intelligently upon a specific arena of pastoral action, and to offer both reasoned guidance and concrete strategies for that action, the NPPHM was a path-breaking initiative. Today it remains practically *sui generis*, at least for the U.S. Catholic Church.

But the NPPHM is noteworthy for at least two other reasons. One is that, while the final version is an official document promulgated by the U.S. bishops, it was informed and shaped by an extensive process of consultation, involving thousands of people – hierarchy, religious professionals, lay leaders and grass-roots folk – over a period of several years. The Plan may well be the most truly collaborative ecclesiastical document ever composed in American Catholicism. Secondly, the NPPHM makes an explicit effort to understand and include the cultural data of the Hispanic people in formulating its directives. Targeted at a cultural milieu with distinct characteristics, the NPPHM purports to be an attempt to define and promote an authentically inculturated pastoral praxis.

How well it succeeds in that attempt is the basic question to be investigated here. The central thrust of this project is an analysis of the way in which culture is handled theologically in the NPPHM, and a critique of this analysis from a perspective informed by the contemporary literature on inculturation. Among the guiding questions are these: how are culture and faith, and their interaction, understood in the Plan? How does the praxis proposed in the Plan flow from its theological presuppositions about the conversation between faith and culture? How, and to what extent, are the relevant data of culture honored and allowed to shape the pastoral strategies that are endorsed? How is the NPPHM to be evaluated as an instance of contextual pastoral theology? Of particular interest here is one of the chief pastoral strategies embraced in the Plan: the development of small ecclesial communities (SECs). This project asks: why? How was this conclusion arrived at? How does the Plan envision that SECs provide a strategic structural platform for authentic inculturation of the faith in the U.S. Hispanic context?

This project is important for a number of reasons. The NPPHM is a crucial blueprint for Roman Catholic pastoral ministry among the Hispanic population of the U.S. From many viewpoints it is manifestly clear that Catholic pastoral praxis has been failing to meet the needs of the Hispanic people in the United States. Historically, as we shall see, Hispanics have been treated as second-class citizens within the U.S. Catholic Church, and have often been marginalized or ignored. A serious hemorrhage of Hispanic Catholics has been underway for some time now, as fundamentalist and pentecostal Protestant churches, Mormons and various sects attract increasing numbers. Moreover, most analysts believe that this already sizeable minority will become the majority within American Catholicism early in

---

3. National Conference of Catholic Bishops, *National Pastoral Plan for Hispanic Ministry* (Washington: USCC, 1988); hereafter referred to as "the NPPHM" or "the Plan." The text first appeared in *Origins* 17:26 (10 Dec. 1987) 449-63.

the twenty-first century. In addition, some of the proposals advanced in the Plan are currently being extensively pursued and giving concrete shape to the experience of the Church; this is especially the case with the widespread development of SECs. In sum, the Roman Catholic Church has a huge stake in the success of the Plan.

But the implications of this study go far beyond the Hispanic context. On the face of it, the NPPHM represents a novel initiative within the U.S. Catholic Church, not only in its adoption of cultural analysis, but in its consultative method of formulation and in the very idea of pastoral planning itself. The NPPHM is already being looked to as a possible model for the development of pastoral plans for other contexts. Such planning is becoming more and more common at the parish and diocesan levels, among religious communities and within particular ministries (e.g., hospital pastoral care, religious education, etc.). Pressure is being exerted for more such efforts at the regional, national and even international levels.

In the NPPHM the bishops called for a periodic appraisal of the Plan's implementation, but to date this has not been done in any systematic way on the national level. Such an assessment would properly require both qualitative and quantitative research on a huge scale, and thus falls outside the scope of this project. Nonetheless, on its own terms the NPPHM document involves some theological issues of fundamental importance. The Plan entails practical strategies with decisive ramifications both for the church and for people's lives. The implications of these issues transcend the specific context for which the Plan is designed. For all these reasons, the NPPHM deserves the critical attention of the academy and the wider church.

Methodology

A complex array of methodological considerations impinge upon pastoral studies of the kind undertaken here. This makes the question of methodology in pastoral theological research an unavoidably thorny one. A plurality of methods obtains in this discipline, and consensus on appropriate method in a particular case is often impossible to achieve. In sum, the pastoral theologian benefits from acquaintance with a variety of hermeneutical and pastoral theologies.

This project represents an effort to evaluate the nature and quality of the conversation between faith and culture in the NPPHM. And, because correlational theology is dialogical by nature, it is also necessarily hermeneutical. This project is thus an exercise in practical hermeneutics. It attempts to assess the meaning of a document, the NPPHM, as one moment within an ongoing pastoral praxis. To do so, it brings to bear the hermeneutical lenses proffered by Tracy, Robert Schreiter and others. These sources suggest that praxis – as distinguished from mere practice – has a *telos*, or goal, toward which it intends to move. That goal may be succinctly described as the "integral liberation"[4] of the human person. The NPPHM itself purports to aim at that lofty goal through the strategies it adopts. Tracy, Schreiter, et al. may help us discern whether and to what degree the Plan succeeds.

The Plan will be evaluated with regard to the largest Hispanic cohort, the Mexican Americans. To reach its goals the study must first attempt to grasp an understanding of the Mexican American cultural situation. A phenomenological description of that culture is laid out, drawing primarily from Mexican American sources. Then the NPPHM is situated within the history of American Catholicism. The Plan's lineage is traced from previous official statements targeted at the Hispanic context, through the consultative *Encuentro* processes. In addition, there exists some secondary literature reflecting upon the NPPHM. These sources will be augmented by a small amount of interview material conducted with people who were personally and directly involved in the process of the formulation of the Plan. Taken together, these texts should amply illumine the nature, origins and status of the NPPHM.

The study examines the text of the NPPHM in some detail. This includes its structure and movement, with attention to the interaction of theory and practice at work in the document. Special focus will be given to its treatment of culture in general, and the Mexican American cultural milieu in particular. After assessing the internal coherence of the text, the project evaluates the document against both the theology of inculturation and the cultural data provided.

Contemporary reflection on inculturation rests upon a correlational understanding of theology. Clearly culture, and the modern sociological tools employed to study it, can only be taken with full seriousness as theological sources within a correlational approach to theology. Theologians of inculturation grapple with both the understanding of the concept of culture itself, and the manner in which culture is to be included in theological discourse. Diverse approaches to both are to be found. To seek a definition of culture is to thrust oneself into the fractious world of the social sciences. I shall follow Clifford Geertz in his preference for a "semiotic" concept of culture as a set of "socially established structures of meaning," a "context... within which social events, behaviors, institutions, or processes can be intelligently – that is, thickly – described."[5] Geertz's fuller definition of culture is:

> [Culture] denotes an historically transmitted pattern of meanings embodied in symbols, a system of inherited conceptions expressed in symbolic forms by means of

---

4. Congregation for the Doctrine of the Faith, "Instruction on Christian Freedom and Liberation" (22 March 1986), esp. #63; Alfred T. Hennelly, ed., *Liberation Theology: A Documentary History* (Maryknoll, N.Y.: Orbis, 1990), p. 481.

5. *The Interpretation of Cultures*, (N.Y.: Basic Books, 1973), pp. 5, 12, 14.

which [humans] communicate, perpetuate, and develop their knowledge about and attitudes toward life. [89]

In a well-known essay, Geertz described religion as a "cultural system."[6] Geertz's approach to "cultural systems" has attracted wide attention and offers important possibilities for contemporary theological reflection.[7]

For the manner of including cultural data, this study will depend primarily on theologian Robert Schreiter's *Constructing Local Theology*,[8] to which we shall turn in the next section. Methodologically, Schreiter offers the pastoral theological researcher a structure within which to bring faith and culture together as conversation partners. Schreiter's model will be employed to assess the strengths and weaknesses of the NPPHM as an authentically inculturated local theology. Most of the conclusions arrived at in this study will be generated through the application of Schreiter's mapping technique to the NPPHM.

Thus, in sum, the methodology of the project is correlational and hermeneutical, and its procedure is threefold: phenomenological, analytical and evaluative. Interpretation of the meaning of the Plan by historical narrative and analysis yields to critique of the Plan from the perspective of a correlational theology of inculturation. The evaluative conclusions of the study are suggestive of some reflections on the prospects and problems for implementation of the Plan. These remarks may indicate both further questions and study, as well as possible implications and applications for other fields.

Inculturation

Culture is both a problem and a resource for Christianity. The question of how Christians are to relate to the social context is as old as the Christian mission itself. H. Richard Niebuhr's seminal *Christ and Culture* effectively attests to the enduring nature of the questions and the variety of responses they have received from the Christian community in various contexts. "Christian perplexity in this area has been perennial,"[9] says the author. Niebuhr delineated the basic problem in terms of a dynamic interaction between the Christ of faith and the inescapable exigencies of culture. Through the use of a typological approach, he lucidly identified some of the major paradigms on the spectrum of Christian responses to culture. A history of Christian mission, though too long to be undertaken here, would demonstrate the recurring nature of Niebuhr's motifs.[10]

---

6. "Religion as a Cultural System," in *The Interpretation of Cultures*, pp. 87-125.

7. See Carl F. Starkloff, "Inculturation and Cultural Systems," *Theological Studies* 55 (1994) 66-81, 274-94.

8. Maryknoll, N.Y.: Orbis, 1985. Schreiter himself depends heavily on Geertz; see especially pp. 53-6.

9. H. R. Niebuhr, *Christ and Culture* (N.Y.: Harper & Row, 1951), p. 2.

10. See Louis J. Luzbetak, *The Church and Cultures*, rev. ed. (Maryknoll, N.Y.: Orbis, 1988).

The Second Vatican Council propelled Roman Catholic thinking about the relationship in new directions. Pope John XXIII himself, who stunned the world with his unexpected convocation of an ecumenical council, then set the tone for the Council's efforts in his remarkable opening statement to the assembly. After affirming that Catholic doctrine must be updated through modern research methods and re-articulated in modern language, he made the controversial claim that "the substance of the ancient deposit of faith is one thing, and the way in which it is presented is another."[11] In effect, the pope admitted that the Church's dogmatic expressions were culturally conditioned, and he implicitly invited reexamination and reformulation of that heritage in accord with a diversity of cultural perspectives.

The composition of the Council comprises an extraordinary fact in itself. Among the 2,500 Council Fathers were significant numbers of native prelates from Asia, Africa and Latin America, in addition to the preponderance of Europeans and North Americans. It was this representation of diverse cultures from far-flung parts of the globe that so impressed Karl Rahner and many other observers. Indeed, Rahner considered Vatican II the most significant council to be convened since the first century. He saw the Council standing at the threshold of a "third epoch" inaugurating, however partially and imperfectly, the consciousness and operation of "the world Church."[12]

A cursory examination of the Council's major documents reveals several interesting things. The terms "inculturation" and "contextualization" never appear in the documents, of course; both are neologisms of the postconciliar era. The words "culture(s)" and "cultural" appear only three times in the document that was intended to be the centerpiece of the Council's work, *Lumen Gentium*, the *Dogmatic Constitution on the Church*. Similarly, the terms are found only twice in *Nostra Aetate*, the *Declaration on the Church's Relation to Non-Christian Religions*; twice in *Sacrosanctum Concilium*, the *Constitution on the Sacred Liturgy*; and once each in *Unitatis Redintegratio*, the *Decree on Ecumenism*; *Dignitatis Humanae*, the *Declaration on Religious Freedom*; and *Dei Verbum*, the *Dogmatic Constitution on Divine Revelation*.

However, "culture" and its derivatives appear a fulsome twenty times in *Ad Gentes*, the *Decree on the Church's Missionary Activity*, and a remarkable 84 times in what has become the Council's most memorable contribution, *Gaudium et Spes*, the *Pastoral Constitution on the Church in the World of Today*. It is not incidental that these latter two documents were among the last promulgated, suggesting a

---

11. October 11, 1962; as quoted by A. Shorter, *Toward a Theology of Inculturation* (Maryknoll, N.Y.: Orbis, 1988), p. 188.

12. Karl Rahner, "Towards a Fundamental Theological Interpretation of Vatican II," *Theological Studies* 40 (1979) 716-27. The first epoch identified by Rahner was that of early Jewish Christianity. This was followed by the second epoch, the nineteen centuries of close identification of the Church with Western civilization.

development of interest and thought on the importance of culture within the Council Fathers' theological and pastoral reflection. In the Council's earlier documents a classicist definition of culture, referring mainly to the graphic and performing arts, prevails. In the later documents, especially *Ad Gentes* and *Gaudium et Spes*, a richer and more anthropologically informed usage becomes the norm.

Ad Gentes' clear call for the study of cultures, leading to "a more profound adaptation" [#22] of the Gospel in mission lands, has been enormously important in the postconciliar renewal of mission theology. Indeed it "ushered in a new epoch in mission work."[13] But the document has vast implications not only for missiology but also for the Church's own self-understanding as a faith household of plural cultural expressions.

The evolution of that self-understanding came into fuller view in *Gaudium et Spes*. The *Pastoral Constitution on the Church in the World of Today* is justly revered for opening new avenues of dialogue between the church and the plurality of world cultures. Its famous opening paragraph places the church's mission squarely in the midst of humanity's diverse circumstances and struggles:

> The joys and hopes and the sorrows and anxieties of people today, especially of those who are poor and afflicted, are also the joys and hopes, sorrows and anxieties of the disciples of Christ, and there is nothing truly human which does not also affect them. Their community is composed of people united in Christ who are directed by the holy Spirit in their pilgrimage towards the Father's kingdom and who have received the message of salvation to be communicated to everyone. For this reason it feels itself closely linked to the human race and its history.[14]

Dialogue and discernment are implied in the document's well-known dictum of the church's "duty in every age of examining the signs of the times and interpreting them in the light of the gospel." [#4] An entire chapter was devoted to "The Proper Development of Culture." One commentator says of this chapter, "The inclusion of culture as a theme and the approach taken form perhaps the most innovative section of the whole document."[15] The influence of twentieth-century cultural anthropology upon this section is quite plain. The document highlights the human importance of culture, especially in its religious dimension:

---

13. Carl F. Starkloff, "Commentary on the Decree on the Church's Missionary Activity," in George P. Schner, ed., *The Church Renewed: The Documents of Vatican II Reconsidered* (Lanham, MD: University Press of America, 1986), p. 131.

14. *Gaudium et Spes* #1. All citations from the documents of Vatican II are taken from the edition of Norman P. Tanner, *Decrees of the Ecumenical Councils*, vol. 2 (Washington: Georgetown University Press, 1990), pp. 817-1135.

15. Michael Stogre, "Commentary on the *Pastoral Constitution on the Church in the Modern World*," in Schner, ed., *The Church Renewed*, p. 26.

The term "culture" in general refers to everything by which we perfect and develop our many spiritual and physical endowments; applying ourselves through knowledge and effort to bring the earth within our power; developing ways of behaving and institutions, we make life in society more human, whether in the family or in the civil sphere as a whole; in the course of time we express, share and preserve in our works great spiritual experiences and aspirations to contribute to the progress of many people, even of the whole human race. [#53]

In taking up the question of the relationship between religious faith and culture *Gaudium et Spes* makes some of its most important contributions to an emerging theology of inculturation. The document notes the "many connections between the announcement of salvation and human culture." Divine revelation is seen to be itself culturally conditioned:

In revealing himself to his people, even to the extent of showing himself fully in the incarnate Son, God has spoken in terms of the culture peculiar to different ages.[#58]

Similarly, the Church has existed in many different milieux and

...has adopted the discoveries of various cultures to spread and explain the news of Christ in its preaching to all nations, to explore it and understand it more deeply, and to express it better in liturgical celebration and in the life of the varied community of the faithful. [#58]

The Council made this all-important assertion:

The church, which has been sent to all peoples of whatever age and region, is not connected exclusively or inseparably to any race or nation, to any particular pattern of human behaviour, or to any ancient or recent customs. Loyal to its own tradition and at the same time conscious of its universal mission, it is able to enter into a communion with different forms of culture which enriches both the church and the various cultures.[#58]

In the process of entering into a culture, the Christian message is seen to be an interior agent of cultural renewal, purification and elevation:

The good news of Christ continually renews the life and behaviour of fallen humanity and attacks and dispels the errors and evils which flow from the ever-threatening seduction of sin. It ceaselessly purifies and enhances the ways of peoples. As if from the inside, it enriches with heavenly resources, strengthens, completes and restores in Christ the spiritual endowments and talents of every people and age. [#58]

Moreover, the Council issued an important invitation to theologians:

> Recent studies and discoveries in science, history and philosophy give rise to new enquiries with practical implications, and also demand new investigations by theologians. Moreover, while respecting the methods and requirements of theological science, theologians are invited continually to look for a more appropriate way of communicating doctrine to the people of their time; since there is a difference between the deposit or truths of faith and the manner in which – with their sense and meaning being preserved – they are expressed. [#62]

The Council's embrace of the distinction between faith and faith's culturally conditioned expression is crucial. Coupled with this distinction, the invitation to theological investigation on the basis of the progress of human knowledge presents a virtual charter for the theology of inculturation.

The advances of the Council began to bear fruit almost immediately. An important milestone in continuing development occurred with the 1974 Synod of Bishops, which had focused on the theme of evangelization. It was on the basis of this meeting that Paul VI composed the Apostolic Exhortation *Evangelii Nuntiandi: On Evangelization in the Modern World.*[16] The pope offered some penetrating reflections on the complexities of evangelizing cultures. In one important passage he says:

> The Gospel, and therefore evangelization, are certainly not identical with culture, and they are independent in regard to all cultures. Nevertheless, the Kingdom which the Gospel proclaims is lived by men who are profoundly linked to a culture, and the building up of the Kingdom cannot avoid borrowing the elements of human culture or cultures. Though independent of cultures, the Gospel and evangelization are not necessarily incompatible with them; rather they are capable of permeating them all without becoming subject to any one of them.
>
> The split between the Gospel and culture is without a doubt the drama of our time, just as it was of other times. Therefore, every effort must be made to ensure a full evangelization of culture, or more correctly of cultures. They have to be regenerated by an encounter with the Gospel. But this encounter will not take place if the Gospel is not proclaimed. [#20]

The pope described evangelization as a process of discrete phases: assimilation, transposition and proclamation. The important passage is worth citing at length:

> The individual Churches, intimately built up not only of people but also of aspirations, of riches and limitations, of ways of praying, of loving, of looking at life and the world, which distinguish this or that human gathering, have the task of

---

16. Washington: USCC, 1975.

assimilating the essence of the Gospel message and of transposing it, without the slightest betrayal of its essential truth, into the language that these particular people understand, then of proclaiming it in this language.

The transposition has to be done with the discernment, seriousness, respect and competence which the matter calls for in the field of liturgical expression, and in the areas of catechesis, theological formulation, secondary ecclesial structures, and ministries. And the word "language" should be understood here less in the semantic or literary sense than in the sense which one may call anthropological and cultural.

The question is undoubtedly a delicate one. Evangelization loses much of its force and effectiveness if it does not take into consideration the actual people to whom it is addressed, if it does not use their language, their signs and symbols, if it does not answer the questions they ask, and if it does not have an impact on their concrete life. But on the other hand, evangelization risks losing its power and disappearing altogether if one empties or adulterates its content under the pretext of translating it; if, in other words, one sacrifices this reality and destroys the unity without which there is no universality, out of a wish to adapt a universal reality to a local situation. [#62]

Paul VI's thought in *Evangelii Nuntiandi* was cautious and carefully nuanced. Aylward Shorter, one of the leading theologians of inculturation, salutes this document as "the fullest and most positive, official statement of the magisterium on inculturation," offering "an advanced theology of a multicultural Church which has probably not been surpassed by any other official statement." [214f.]   The document's effect was to encourage further discussion, not only of evangelization, but of the character of the Church and its mission. In addition, *Evangelii Nuntiandi* gave critical affirmation to the rapidly expanding development of small Christian communities as tools of evengelization.

On the eve of the Second Vatican Council, Jesuit missiologist Joseph Masson had spoken of the urgent need for an "inculturated Catholicism."[17] The appearance of the term *inculturation* on the theological landscape is, however, generally attributed to the Jesuit Superior General, Fr. Pedro Arrupe, who propelled reflection forward in a memorable 1978 letter to the order. Arrupe began with this description of inculturation often quoted in subsequent literature:

Inculturation is the incarnation of Christian life and of the Christian message in a particular cultural context, in such a way that this experience not only finds expression through elements proper to the culture in question (this alone would be no more than

---

17. J. Masson, "L'Eglise ouverte sur le monde," *Nouvelle Revue Théologique* 84:10 (Dec. 1962) 1038. Cf. also J. Masson, "La mission à la lumière de l'Incarnation," *Nouvelle Revue Théologique* 98:10 (Dec. 1976) 865-90.

a superficial adaptation), but becomes a principle that animates, directs and unifies the culture, transforming it so as to bring about "a new creation."[18]

Drawing upon *Gaudium et Spes, Evangelii Nuntiandi* and the Jesuit community's own experience with cultural diversity, Arrupe envisioned a process that was deep, dialogical and transformative. In that process, which can include elements of confrontation, the Gospel acts from within a culture as an agent of change and renewal. The process involves the assimilation of "universal values which no one culture can exhaustively realize." [3] The result is not only a new cultural synthesis, but new bonds of communion among cultures in a "robe of many colors." [3]

Importantly, Arrupe saw the process of inculturation as located neither in Rome nor in the countries which send missionaries, but in the local church. As the primary agent of inculturation, it is the local church, rooted in a particular culture, which "accepting the past with discernment, constructs the future with its present resources." [2] Moreover, the General stressed that due to the rapid pace of modern cultural change, the need for an inculturated faith was universal and ongoing, embracing historically Christian cultures as well as those receiving the Gospel more recently. He thus placed the nations of the Third World, the "mission lands," on an equal footing with those of the West. [2]

Arrupe's letter was followed rather shortly by Pope John Paul II's embrace of the term *inculturation* in his 1979 Apostolic Exhortation *Catechesi Tradendae: Catechesis in Our Time.*[19] This was the first instance in which *inculturation* made an appearance in an official magisterial document. John Paul explains:

> The term *inculturation* may be a neologism, but it expresses very well one factor of the great mystery of the Incarnation. We can say of catechesis, as well as of evangelization in general, that it is called to bring the power of the Gospel into the very heart of culture and cultures. For this purpose, catechesis will seek to know these cultures and their essential components; it will learn their most significant expressions; it will respect their particular values and riches. In this manner it will be able to offer

---

18. Pedro Arrupe, "To the Whole Society," *Studies in the International Apostolate of Jesuits* 7:1 (June 1978) 2. For fuller treatment of the history of the term *inculturation*, see Nicolas Standaert, S.J., "L'histoire d'un néologisme," *Nouvelle Revue Théologique* 110 (1988) 555-70; and François Guillemette, "L'apparition du concept d'inculturation: Une réception de Vatican II," *Mission* 2:1 (1995) 53-78.

Inculturation must be distinguished from its linguistic cousins. *Enculturation*, for example, is an anthropological term which refers to the process by which an individual is formed or assimilated into a culture. *Acculturation*, also drawn from anthropology, refers to all the phenomena associated with encounter between disparate cultures. *Inculturation*, meanwhile, includes a theological element significant to the church. Shorter defines *inculturation* simply as "the on-going dialogue between faith and culture or cultures." [11]

19. In Austin Flannery, ed., *Vatican Council II: More Postconciliar Documents*, vol. II (Boston: St. Paul Editions, 1982).

these cultures the knowledge of the hidden mystery and help them to bring forth from their own living tradition original expressions of Christian life, celebration and thought. [#53]

At around the same time, two seminal articles appeared by the Dutch theologian Arij A. Roest Crollius, S.J. In the first, "What Is So New about Inculturation?,"[20] Crollius described the process of inculturation in this way:

> The inculturation of the Church is the integration of the Christian experience of a local Church into the culture of its people, in such a way that this experience not only expresses itself in elements of this culture, but becomes a force that animates, orients and innovates this culture so as to create a new unity and communion, not only within the culture in question, but also as an enrichment of the Church universal. [15]

While Crollius' description closely parallels that of Arrupe, the addition of the final phrase strengthens the view of the exchange as one of mutual enrichment. Inculturation is a two-way street upon which the Church not only gives but receives something as well.

Crollius saw the process of inculturation unfolding in three interconnected and ongoing moments. The first could be called the moment of "translation," or acculturation, in which "the Church comes into contact with a new culture, presenting the Christian message and life in the forms of another culture." In a second moment, usually characterized by the stability and growth of a local community, the Church is becoming more deeply "assimilated" to the thought and forms of the receiving culture. In the final moment, the Church gradually assumes a more active role in the "transformation" of the culture and, complementarily, is itself the object of transformation. [14]

In answering the question, therefore, "What is so new about inculturation?," Crollius had begun with the admission that, on one level, nothing at all is new about it, insofar as Christianity has been interacting with cultures from its very beginning. However, he identified three new elements in the contemporary situation which lie behind the coinage of a new term, *inculturation.* One is the greater awareness of the dialogical character of the interaction between the Church and culture, especially of the aspect by which the Church itself is affected and enhanced. The reciprocal character of the process is insufficiently comprehended by such formerly popular terms as *adaptation* and *accommodation.* A second factor is that the concept of *inculturation* more adequately recognizes and guides the pivotal role played by the local church. It is thus a useful notion in every context, not just in the

---

20. *Gregorianum* 59 (1978) 721-738. This article was later reprinted in A. Crollius and Théoneste Nkéramihigo, *What Is So New about Inculturation?*, vol. V of the series *Inculturation* (Rome: Pontifical Gregorian University, 1984); page number citations here are from the reprint.

"young churches" of the Third World. Finally, *inculturation* reflects a more inductive, descriptive, anthropologically informed conception of *culture* itself. [16f.]

Crollius wrestled with the third matter, the problem of defining culture, more extensively in a later article, "Inculturation and the Meaning of Culture."[21] Guided by the theological anthropology of fellow Jesuits Karl Rahner and A. van Leeuwen, Crollius found Geertz's definition of culture highly serviceable in all but one crucial respect, namely, the problem of cultural diversity and interaction. On this point Crollius turned to the work of David Tracy and others on the concept of "analogy" to open an understanding of the possibilities of cross-cultural communication. On this view, Crollius concluded beautifully:

> The purpose of inculturation is not to salvage a traditional culture, but rather to render present in the galloping process of change which affects all cultures the light and the life of the Gospel, so that each culture may become a worthy "habitat" of God's pilgrim people – a tent rather than a fortress – and an irradiating light that adds to the splendor of the entire cosmos. [54]

The author was grasping toward a dynamic, rather than static, view of culture, one that was respectful of cultural change, originality and particularity, yet optimistic about the potential for intercultural conversation.

Both official teaching and theological thinking have continued to mature. In 1988 Aylward Shorter produced the most comprehensive Roman Catholic treatment of the subject to date, *Toward a Theology of Inculturation*. Pope John Paul II has returned to the theme on a number of occasions, most notable among them his 1990 encyclical *Redemptoris Missio: On the Permanent Validity of the Church's Missionary Mandate.*[22] Here the pontiff reiterated that inculturation is "not a matter of purely external adaptation," but "a profound and all-embracing process." [#52] He also affirmed that inculturation is a reciprocal process, saying:

> Through inculturation the Church makes the Gospel incarnate in different cultures and at the same time introduces peoples, together with their cultures, into her own community. She transmits to them her own values, at the same time taking the good elements that already exist in them and renewing them from within. Through inculturation the Church, for her part, becomes a more intelligible sign of what she is, and a more effective instrument of mission. [#52]

---

21. *Gregorianum* 61 (1980) 253-74; reprinted in Crollius and Nkéramihigo, op. cit. Page number citations are from the reprint.

22. Washington: USCC, 1990. Also noteworthy is John Paul's encyclical *Slavorum Apostoli: In Commemoration of the Evangelizing Work of Saints Cyril and Methodius* (Boston: St. Paul Editions, 1985), in which he held up the two apostles of the Slavs as exemplars of inculturation.

The pope cautioned that authentic inculturation proceeds slowly and deliberately, and entails commitments to ecumenical and interfaith dialogue, and work for all forms economic development and social justice.

Evaluating Local Theology

In 1985 Robert J. Schreiter's important book *Constructing Local Theologies* appeared. Schreiter displayed a preference for the terminology of *contextual theology* and *contextualization*. His hesitation about usage of the term *inculturation* rests on the perception that "it causes some difficulties in dialogue with social scientists in that it seems to be a dilettantish kind of neologism on the part of non-scientists." [5] Although he admits that *contextual theology* is also a neologism, he claims that this term "has the advantage of not having many previous associations and of being readily used in translation into a wide variety of languages." [6] Clearly, however, when Schreiter speaks of *contextual* or *local theology* as the product of dynamic interaction among gospel, church and culture, he is referring to the same process resulting in what elsewhere would be called an inculturated theology.

Schreiter saw local theology unfolding according to three groups of models – translation, adaptation and contextual. Translation models, generally the first to be used in pastoral settings, depend upon a "kernel and husk" understanding of Christianity in which it is thought that the core Gospel message can be separated from its cultural "husk." Schreiter objects that this both disembodies revelation and fails to take the receiving culture seriously enough. Adaptation models, while they strive to understand the local culture more deeply through the use of philosophy or the social sciences, often end up forcing the data of culture into foreign categories. In addition, says Schreiter, these approaches still tend to remove the Christian message itself from its cultural settings, and they tend to operate in a one-way, rather than reciprocal, manner.

Among contextual models the author identifies two different types. The first he calls the "ethnographic" approach. Here the emphasis is upon defining and defending cultural identity. Although this has obvious advantages, says the author, such an approach can also fall prey to cultural romanticism or over-reliance upon experts, and it may ignore conflictual factors at work in a given situation. The second type, the "liberation" approach, highlights oppressive aspects of a situation and focuses on the need for change. Doing so can bring to bear the salvific aspects of the gospel in a particularly powerful way in concrete social circumstances, although the liberation models can succumb to the pitfalls of over-reliance upon Marxist analysis or other apocalyptic ideologies. "Liberation theologies," concludes the author, "are a major force, if not the major force, in contextual models of theology today." [15]

Schreiter claims that the contemporary rise of "local theologies" is "pointing the way to a return to theology as an occasional enterprise, that is, one dictated by circumstances and immediate needs rather than the need for system-building." [23] He provides a way to "map" the development of local theology, an idealized picture of the inculturation process as a nine-step interaction between church tradition, on the one hand, and culture on the other. [23-36] (See illustration next page.) The author offers this mapping technique as a tool to local communities both for purposes of locating themselves in the process and for evaluating the adequacy and completeness of their theological efforts.

Schreiter stresses that the construction of local theology never begins in a vacuum. Every local community bears a heritage, a lived spirituality or popular religiosity, expressed in an already-existing local theology that may be more or less explicit, complete and coherent. The process of constructing or revising local theologybegins, says Schreiter, when the heritage is experienced to be inadequate. Dissatisfaction with the existing local theology can be triggered by the community's own growth in reflective awareness, by the intrusion of a social event or cultural condition, or by the community coming into contact with theological efforts from other cultures or larger ecclesial structures.

Ideally, according to Schreiter, the next step in the process consists of what he calls the "opening of culture." [28] This involves careful listening to a culture through any of several means of analysis. In a later chapter Schreiter makes clear his preference for a semiotic approach to culture, as in the work of Clifford Geertz. Theologically, Schreiter emphasizes that listening to culture hinges on the conviction that Christ is already present to and active in the culture, and not simply something the Church brings from the outside. The study of a culture results in the identification of "culture texts," signs or series of signs of pivotal importance to that culture. These signs provide resources for the third step, the emergence of key themes for local theology.

On the other side of the dialogue is the faith tradition borne by the Church, and in the fourth step this tradition undergoes a process of opening parallel to the opening of culture. The analysis of tradition should be not only historical but open to the plurality of cultures encompassed by the tradition. Furthermore, in the fifth movement, the tradition is regarded as itself a series of local theologies to which hermeneutics of suspicion and retrieval must be applied.[23] To amplify this perspective, Schreiter explores the many different forms which theology has taken over the centuries. He groups them into four large categories: theology as

---

23. As Shorter says, the Church's "patrimony" is inherently multicultural, "the legacies of multiple past inculturations." [*Toward a Theology of Inculturation*, p. 256.] This is echoed by J. Scheuer: "The whole history of the Church, the history of the Christian communities since their origins, can be considered as the history of the *inculturation of the Christian faith* in particular societies and cultures." ["Inculturation: Presentation of the Topic," *Lumen Vitae* 40:1 (1985) 16.]

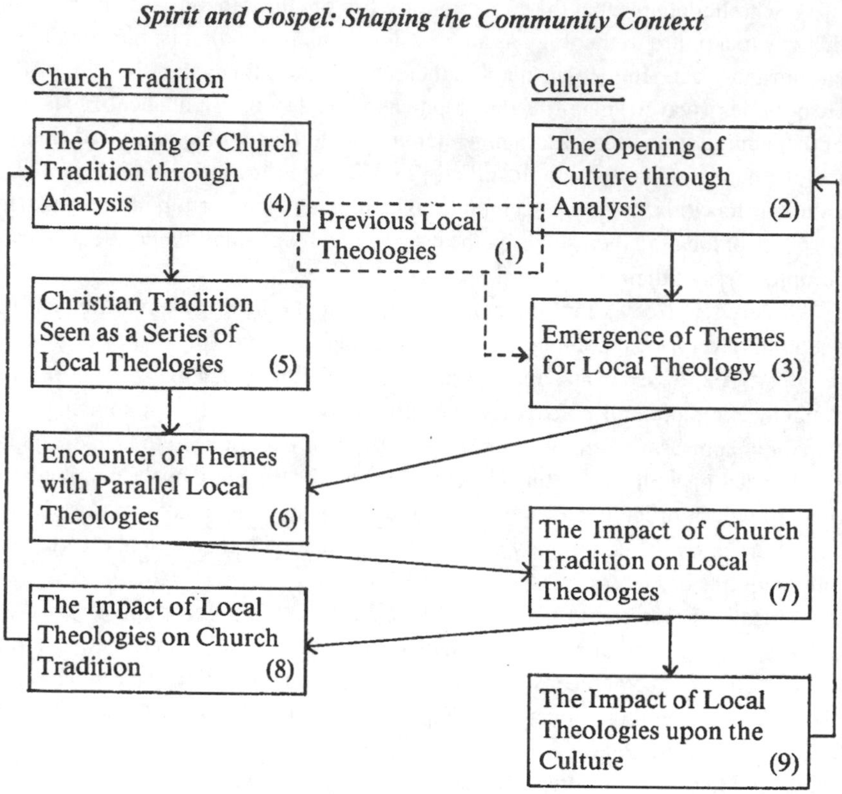

Spirit and Gospel: Shaping the Community Context

Church Tradition   Culture

The Opening of Church Tradition through Analysis (4)	The Opening of Culture through Analysis (2)

Previous Local Theologies   (1)

Christian Tradition Seen as a Series of Local Theologies (5)	Emergence of Themes for Local Theology (3)

Encounter of Themes with Parallel Local Theologies (6)	
	The Impact of Church Tradition on Local Theologies (7)
The Impact of Local Theologies on Church Tradition (8)	
	The Impact of Local Theologies upon the Culture (9)

[Figure 1. From *Constructing Local Theologies*, p. 25.]

variations on a sacred text, theology as wisdom, theology as sure knowledge and theology as praxis. The variety of forms is correlated with a wide spectrum of cultural and social exigencies.

The development of local theology proper begins in the sixth step, the "encounter of church tradition and local themes." [33] This is where the fruits of steps three and five come together. Schreiter explains: "Local theologies in the church tradition are sought out that parallel the local theme or need, either in content, in context, in form, or in all three." This is followed, seventh, by the "impact of the tradition on local theology." [34] The encounter may offer affirmation to the local theology, and/or it may provide challenge and/or correction to what has been happening locally. Concomitantly, the local theology has an impact on the tradition, the eighth movement. "Local theologies," says Schreiter, "are vital for the development of the tradition." [34] They may serve to remind the rest of us of segments of the tradition that we have forgotten or ignored, and they may serve to improve upon that tradition through their insights into dilemmas experienced analogously by other local churches. Finally, local theologies merge into and have an impact upon their own cultures. They may help to reframe certain issues or rectify certain aspects of the cultural worldview. Conversely, such theologies may also, wittingly or not, bestow other questions or problems on subsequent generations, and these matters may form the basis for later local theological reflection. The process is thus ongoing, dynamic and, in a certain sense, circular.

Throughout his work Schreiter evinces a concern for the maintenance of authentic Christian identity in the development of contextualized theology. This is evident in his description of the steps of the process. It is equally evident in the way he takes up the difficult subjects of popular religion and syncretism in relation to local theology.[24] Most useful to this concern on a practical level, however, are the five criteria Schreiter proposes by which local theologies are to be evaluated vis-a-vis the tradition. [118-20] The first is the test of cohesiveness; a theology must manifest an overall consistency with revelation and tradition. Secondly, the theology must bear a positive affinity with Christian worship and ritual – the ancient principle of *lex orandi, lex credendi*. The third criterion is praxis: what is the performance engendered by the theology, and is it discernibly in accord with the liberating thrust of the Gospel? Fourthly, a local theology must stand under the judgment of other local churches, not rupturing that communion which is the fabric of the universal Church. Lastly, and complementary to the previous criterion, an authentic local theology should impel a local community outward, offering collaboration and challenge to other local churches. A local theology must pass all five of these tests in order to be judged affirmatively.

Widely hailed, *Constructing Local Theologies* is a sophisticated work which rewards careful reading. Schreiter has collected and integrated much of the best thinking of the postconciliar era on the relationship of faith to plural cultures. Equally important, through his mapping technique and the elaboration of testing criteria, Schreiter has provided us with a set of instruments by which to evaluate local theological efforts such as the *National Pastoral Plan for Hispanic Ministry*.

As we have seen, the dialogue between faith and culture is as old as Christianity itself. The terms of this interaction have existed all along, and it can be avoided by neither positivists of religion nor positivists of culture. Historical consciousness, however, and with it consciousness of cultural plurality, has flowered more fully in the modern era. The modern, scientific concept of culture

---

24. *Constructing Local Theologies*, chap. 6, pp. 122-43, and chap. 7, pp. 144-58, respectively; see also Schreiter, "Defining Syncretism: An Interim Report," *International Bulletin of Missionary Research* 17 (April 1993) 50-3.

has stimulated the unfolding of an appreciation that different peoples and groups view life and life's important questions in radically diverse ways. Thus, while it can trace the lineage of its fundamental issues as far back in time as one may go, the theology of inculturation is of comparatively recent origin. The contemporary search for greater clarity in the relatively uncharted territory of cultural diversity continues to unfold.

As awareness of the plurality of cultures and of the cultural conditioning of faith expressions grows, we can expect the theology of inculturation to continue to grow in importance across all branches of the discipline. It will not be surprising if its influence is initially felt most profoundly in the area of pastoral praxis. Pastoral theologians have the task of reflecting upon and adjudicating many competing claims and aspects within concrete pastoral situations, even though they often do so through diverging methods and procedures. Throughout the Christian churches there is a growing awareness of the central place owed to cultural factors in pastoral reflection and planning. Increasingly demands for preaching, catechesis, styles of worship, other forms of pastoral ministry, and even ecclesial structures suited to the cultural ethos of a given people are being heard. It is admitted more readily today that inherited or customary pastoral practice, even if of long duration and even if judged to be sound in one cultural context, may or may not be judged as adequate in another.

A number of examples could be cited here by which we might see this glacial shift taking place within the Roman Catholic Church of the United States. This project focusses on just one, the *National Pastoral Plan for Hispanic Ministry*. The NPPHM reflects an attempt at an upper level of church leadership to come to grips with the challenges and needs of a particular ethnic grouping within the panoply of cultures which is the contemporary U.S.A. Evaluating how well it succeeds in that attempt, from the point of view of the theology of inculturation, utilizing the tools given us by Robert Schreiter, is the goal of this study.

CHAPTER TWO

Mexican Americans:
Cultural Data

Before turning to the Plan itself, we need to inquire into and in some way describe one of the cultural contexts toward which the plan is targeted, namely, those Hispanics identified as Mexican Americans. This is approached in three steps. The first is a brief historical overview of the Mexican American people. This will be followed by a descriptive synopsis of the character and distinctive cultural traits and values of Mexican Americans. Closely linked to that description will be special attention paid to the characteristics of Mexican American popular religiosity. This leads to the third step, an examination of the pastoral situation of Mexican Americans in the U.S., calling attention to both the strengths and the current challenges.

History: *La Raza* Emerges

On a high hill overlooking downtown Mexico City stands an imposing fortress dating from Spanish colonial days. Chapultepec Castle was the site of the final and most tragic engagement of the Mexican-American War. U.S. General Winfield Scott had already ravaged central Mexico and militarily brought Mexico to its knees. Nevertheless, Scott decided to break the armistice of 24 August 1847, when he suspected that the Mexicans were using the cease-fire to reinforce their positions. On 14 September U.S. forces were ordered up the steep slopes of the hill to capture the Mexican stronghold. Barricaded inside the thick walls were not regular Mexican forces, but military cadets, young men mostly in their teens. Although badly outnumbered, short of ammunition and overwhelmed by superior firepower, the cadets by all accounts fought courageously to the last. As American troops breached the walls and stormed the fort, the surviving defenders are said to have jumped out of the castle's windows to their deaths on the rocks below rather than accept defeat and imprisonment by the invading enemy. The blood of these *niños heroes* makes Chapultepec one of Mexico's most revered patriotic shrines.[1]

For Mexicans, and indeed for all Latin Americans, Chapultepec endures as a symbol of resistance to Yankee imperialism. But, if Chapultepec stands as a

---

1. Julian Samora and Patricia Vandel Simon, *A History of the Mexican-American People*, rev. ed. (Notre Dame: U. of Notre Dame Press, 1993), p. 97; also, Rodolfo Acuña, *Occupied America: A History of Chicanos*, 3rd ed. (N.Y.: Harper & Row, 1988), p. 18.

reminder of one of Mexico's proudest and bravest moments, it is not far away from another site that was the scene of national humiliation. The Treaty of Guadalupe Hidalgo, which ended the Mexican-American War, is named after the Mexico City suburb where it was signed on 2 February 1848. Under the terms of this treaty Mexico recognized the 1845 U.S. annexation of Texas, and it relinquished to the United States additional lands which now comprise the states of California, Arizona, New Mexico, Nevada, Utah and parts of Colorado and Wyoming. The sum of the Mexican Cession was more than half of the territory which Mexico had claimed at the time of its independence from Spain in 1821. In return, the U.S. agreed to assume the claims of Americans against Mexico, and to pay Mexico a sum of money. To make matters worse, when the treaty came before the U.S. Senate for ratification, that body unilaterally struck certain provisions from the agreement. Defeated, Mexico had little choice but to accept the terms dictated by its more powerful neighbour.[2]

Guadalupe Hidalgo left a bitter legacy of hostility and suspicion in the relations between Mexico and the U.S. This was aggravated by the fact that some of the provisions of the treaty were not strictly adhered to by the United States. Most notorious in this regard was the matter of the property rights of people living in the ceded territory, rights which the U.S. had pledged to uphold. Original owners were often stripped of their lands as Mexican property laws and documentation were disregarded, or such owners found themselves having to defend their claims in lengthy and costly litigation. In addition, despite treaty assurances, the civil rights of the former Mexicans and their descendants were often trampled, sometimes through legal channels, other times through various methods of social pressure. Harassment of the practice of the Roman Catholic religion and imposition of the English language were not uncommon.[3]

But the Treaty of Guadalupe Hidalgo had one other important consequence: it granted U.S. citizenship to the former Mexican subjects. To be sure, this was for many decades thereafter a second-class citizenship in which Mexicans, like other Hispanics and people of color generally, have been effectively marginated from political and economic power. But henceforth the United States was to be, in fact if not yet in self-understanding, a partly Hispanic nation. Two great cultures intersected in what became the American Southwest. The progeny of their union is the Mexican American people.

For their part, the Mexican Americans brought with them a rich and varied cultural history. Their very identity up to this time was the product of the often-violent collision of European and Mesoamerican cultures begun more than 300 years earlier. When Hernán Cortez overthrew the Aztec empire he brought with

---

2. Samora and Simon, p. 99; Acuña, pp. 19-20.
3. Samora and Simon, pp. 100-2.

him not only deadly Old World diseases, new technologies and drastically different social patterns, but an aggressive form of Christianity, Spanish Catholicism. While the native peoples were both practically and conceptually unprepared for this cultural encounter, the Spanish brought with them a ready-made distinction between *barbarian* and *civilized* peoples. They regarded the conquered peoples as of the former type and themselves as under a sacred obligation to spread civilization. This gave the Spanish a religious rationale for consolidating their military conquests. In the Spanish view, the process of civilization consisted not so much in replacing existing, functioning cultural institutions, but in filling a perceived void. Thus, Spanish cultural assumptions were such that they expected the Indians to be passive, even grateful recipients of effective government, true religion and European cultural refinements.[4]

The introduction of Christianity among the native peoples of Mexico and the Southwest proceeded by various means. In some cases the Spaniards resorted to the application of military force and direct imposition of Spanish ways on the vanquished peoples. More often the indigenous peoples' first contacts with Christianity came about in one of two ways. The first was through the new economic order fostered by the Spanish, centered in the colonial town. Here the Indians were often recruited as labor for the agricultural estates and mines. Although never legally enslaved, native labor was often forced, conditions were harsh, and native people found themselves excluded from Spanish society as far as possible. In general, then, life in the colonial towns represented for these peoples a drastic break with former cultural patterns and submission to domination by foreigners. At the same time, however, the intermingling of races and cultures was taking place largely between the Indians and the poorer class of Spanish immigrants.[5]

The other avenue of cultural interaction was the mission community, and it presented a quite different social world for the native peoples. One must be very careful, of course, to avoid popular romanticization or exaggeration of the positive aspects of mission life. Conditions in the missions were often very harsh also, and white cruelty could be delivered through the hands of a Franciscan or Jesuit as well as through the mine owner or chief of the presidio. The "reduction" of native people to the life of a compact village surrounding a church, under the autocratic rule of a missionary priest, represented a huge change in lifestyle for most of the native peoples. Still, the mission structure afforded some degree of protection from secular Spanish encroachment, and some measure of preservation of native identity and culture. Old ways were gradually modified in a communal setting. Cultural transfer took place under the coercion of mission discipline, to be sure, but also

---

4. Edward H. Spicer, *Cycles of Conquest: The Impact of Spain, Mexico, and the United States on the Indians of the Southwest, 1533-1960* (Tucson: University of Arizona Press, 1962), pp. 281-2.

5. Spicer, pp. 298-306.

through preaching, catechesis, religious ritual and the economic benefits accruing to Spanish agricultural techniques, crafts and trade. At their best, the mission communities provided a context for profound acculturation without obliterating native cultures altogether.[6]

The first Spanish missionary and colonizing efforts on the northern frontier of New Spain had begun before the close of the 16th century in the Rio Grande Valley. Never large in numbers, and only modestly successful in evangelizing the native peoples of the area, the colonial communities of New Mexico persisted despite isolation and hardship. Mission communities in Texas were founded only in the last decade of the 17th century, and in upper California in the middle and latter 1700s. Among all these the California communities founded by Junipero Serra (1713-1784) and other Franciscans became the most successful and economically prosperous. However, by the time of the Mexican-American War the entire mission system in the Southwest was in a state of serious decline. The secularization of the missions in 1835 culminated a long period of isolation and neglect by both Spain and Mexico.[7]

The Anglo invasion of the Southwest began early in the 19th century. A lucrative, if often illegal, trade was opened up over the Santa Fe Trail. Merchants were followed by settlers. Just as important as trade goods and hunger for land, the American merchants and settlers came armed with the aggressive ideology of "Manifest Destiny," a dream of extending U.S. territory from coast to coast. Stephen Austin led his band of Missourians into Texas in 1821, opening twenty-five years of turmoil in that region. As events unfolded in Texas, New Mexico and California, American subversion fueled unrest and conflict. Texas statehood and a minor border dispute were all it took to ignite a war that proved disastrous for Mexico. The Treaty of Guadalupe Hidalgo fulfilled the aspirations of American expansionism spectacularly.[8]

The Anglo influx into the Southwest increased dramatically after the American victory. It was motivated by the gold strike in California the same year as the treaty was signed, the discovery of other resources and, as always, the voracious appetite for land. That migration has continued more or less unabated ever since. The levers of political and economic power throughout the Southwest, as elsewhere, remained almost exclusively in Anglo hands until the 1960s. Historically Mexicans have provided unskilled agricultural and industrial labor, receiving in return low wages, poor schools, inferior housing and social exclusion.

---

6. Spicer, pp. 288-98.
7. Samora and Simon, pp. 50-7; also, Alfredo Mirandé, *The Chicano Experience* (Notre Dame: U. of Notre Dame Press, 1985), pp. 128-31.
8. Samora and Simon, pp. 69-97; Mirandé, pp. 131-7.

Their struggle for justice and self-determination forms one of the great American social narratives of the 20th century.[9]

What the treaty framers of 1848 likely did not foresee were the reciprocal ways in which American society would be profoundly influenced by the Mexican people remaining in the Southwest and their descendants. No doubt some Anglos expected them to simply go away or disappear into the American "melting pot" and become indistinguishable from others. But, to a remarkable degree, through the ties of language, religion and family, Mexican Americans have maintained their identity and culture over the succeeding fifteen decades.

This perseverance is also due in no small part to the continuing migration of Mexicans and other Hispanics into the U.S. over these years. The Mexico-U.S. border has been and remains a porous frontier, despite the best efforts of the Border Patrol. Successive waves of immigrants, both legal and illegal, have crossed that border, joining family members on the other side and looking for refuge and economic opportunity. One such wave occurred during the chaotic years of the Mexican Revolution, 1911-16. By one estimate, nearly ten percent of Mexico's population fled the country during those years of civil unrest.[10] Moreover, the large number of immigrants during those years was more than the economy of the Southwest could absorb. The result was that for the first time significant numbers of Mexican Americans began to move into other regions of the country, especially the large industrial cities of the North.[11]

Tightening of immigration laws in the 1920s and the Great Depression of the 1930s slowed the tide for a time. But the labor shortages brought on by the Second World War lured another large wave of Mexicans across the border.[12] World War II had other important consequences for Mexican Americans. For one thing, it accelerated the dispersal of Mexican Americans throughout the country. More importantly, large numbers of Mexican Americans served with distinction in the armed forces, where they found a relative equality of treatment unknown in civilian life. They were exposed to educational, training and leadership opportunities from which they had largely been shut out previously. After the war, the "G.I. Bill of Rights" allowed them to enter colleges and universities in unprecedented numbers.[13] These experiences fueled postwar aspirations for equality and self-determination

---

9. See, for example, Acuña, esp. pp. 307-62.

10. Samora and Simon, p. 130; they were relying upon Carey McWilliams, *North from Mexico* (Phila.: J. B. Lippincott, 1949), p. 163.

11. Samora and Simon, p. 132.

12. Samora and Simon, pp. 135-40.

13. Samora and Simon, pp. 155-6; also, Moíses Sandoval, "Effects of World War II on the Hispanic People," in Moíses Sandoval, ed., *Fronteras: A History of the Latin American Church in the USA since 1513* (San Antonio: Mexican American Cultural Center, 1983), pp. 341-76.

among Mexican Americans. Their struggle for identity and civil rights has been very public since the 1960s.[14]

The Mexican American people of today are thus a product of a long, often conflictual and still ongoing process of cultural contacts. Mexican American theologian Virgilio Elizondo has expounded the thesis that Mexican American identity can be understood primarily as the fruit of a double *"mestizaje,"*[15] a term which defies facile translation. It signifies the fact or condition of being a racial mixture or hybrid – "the birth of a new people from two preexistent peoples."[16] The first *mestizaje* is a reference to the melding of the Spanish conquerors with the indigenous peoples of Mexico. The symbolic midwife of the first *mestizaje* is *La Morenita*, the Brown Virgin of Guadalupe, whose significance we shall have cause to examine in greater depth shortly. The second *mestizaje* has been underway since the American defeat of Mexico and occupation of the Southwest.

Moreover, Elizondo claims that the Mexican American people have been the object of three evangelizations.[17] The first was by Iberian Catholicism. Secondly came the U.S. Anglo Protestants and French, Irish and German Catholics. More recently Mexican Americans are being evangelized by fundamentalists. "All three evangelizations have proceeded from a conquest paradigm,"[18] says the author. All three tried to suppress or radically transform the culture of the people.

Since *mestizo* peoples tend historically to be disowned and excluded by both parent groups, Mexican Americans find themselves in a double bind, "doubly marginated and rejected."[19] Their history, culture and language have diverged from that of old Mexico; they even find themselves the butt of derogatory terms when they visit that country. On the other hand, their skin color, religion and social status mean they are not accepted as "real" Americans either. "Since the Anglos had a profound disdain for both everything Spanish and everything Indian," says Elizondo, "the Mestizo was looked upon as the mongrel who inherited the worst of

---

14. See David A. Badillo, "Latino/Hispanic History since 1965: The Collective Transformation of Regional Minorities," in Jay P. Dolan and A. F. Deck, eds., *Hispanic Catholic Culture in the U.S.: Issues and Concerns* (Notre Dame: U. of Notre Dame Press, 1994), pp. 50-76, esp. pp. 56-64.

15. V. Elizondo, *Galilean Journey: The Mexican-American Promise* (Maryknoll, N.Y.: Orbis, 1983), pp. 9-18. See also these works by the same author: *Mestizaje: The Dialectic of Cultural Birth and the Gospel* (San Antonio: Mexican American Cultural Center, 1978); "El mestizaje como lugar teológico," in Francisco Moreno Rejón, ed., *Teología y Liberación: Religión, cultura y ética* (Lima, Perú: Instituto Bartolomé de Las Casas, 1991), pp. 13-41; *The Future is Mestizo: Life where Cultures Meet* (N.Y.: Crossroad, 1988); *"Mestizaje* as a Locus of Theological Reflection," in A. F. Deck, ed., *Frontiers of Hispanic Theology in the United States* (Maryknoll, N.Y.: Orbis, 1992), pp. 104-23.

16. *Galilean Journey*, p. 10.

17. "Hispanic Theology and Popular Piety: From Interreligious Encounter to a New Ecumenism," *CTSA Proceedings* 48 (1993) 1-14.

18. "Hispanic Theology and Popular Piety," 6.

19. *Galilean Journey*, p. 20.

two already degenerate peoples."[20] Thus, Mexican Americans have emerged as a unique ethnic entity, *la raza*,[21] as they refer to themselves.

Accordingly, Elizondo and other contemporary spokespersons for Mexican Americans see their people's history largely in terms of oppression and the struggle for liberation from domination.[22] Elizondo summarizes this historical view:

> As a people, we had been born as a result of the U.S. invasion and subsequent conquest of the great northern regions of Mexico from California to Texas. And before that our Mexican ancestors had been born out of the invasion and conquest of pre-Columbian Mexico. As the Spanish conquest of Mexico had tried to suppress everything native, so the Anglo conquest of northern Mexico had tried to suppress and destroy everything Mexican. We could say that in recent historical times, we had been twice conquered, twice victimized, and twice mesticized. Through each conquest, the native soil with its culture and inhabitants had been deeply penetrated but not destroyed. The conquerors had tried to destroy the natives, but in time they would be absorbed and conquered by the product of their own unsuspected creation.[23]

However, Elizondo refuses to see this history in merely tragic or fatalistic terms. For him the *mestizo* identity of the Mexican American people is both a source of richness and "prophetic mission."[24] Indeed, Elizondo thinks that his people are uniquely poised to point the way toward a multicultural future, and to become active agents of evangelization in the modern world.

Religion: Institutional and Popular

Most Mexican Americans, like most other Hispanics, are affiliated in some way with the Roman Catholic Church. The roots of this adherence run deep historically and culturally. The lively and profound faith which so often characterizes Mexican Americans bespeaks a long and, in many ways, successful process of inculturation. One can observe this in liturgical celebrations, in the *fiesta* of Our Lady of Guadalupe, and in the popular religiosity whose evidences are ubiquitous in everyday life. However, at the same time, the story of Mexican American Catholicism is to a great extent a narrative of official neglect and discrimination.

---

20. "Hispanic Theology and Popular Piety," 7.
21. See, e.g., Andrés G. Guerrero, *A Chicano Theology* (Maryknoll, N.Y.: Orbis, 1987), esp. pp. 128-37.
22. *Galilean Journey*, pp.23-7; also, *Christianity and Culture: An Introduction to Pastoral Theology and Ministry for the Bicultural Community* (San Antonio: Mexican American Cultural Center, 1975), pp. 129-53. This is also the perspective of R. Acuña's *Occupied America*, op. cit.
23. *The Future is Mestizo*, p. 39f.
24. *Galilean Journey*, pp. 107-11; *The Future is Mestizo*, pp. 87-111.

The penetration of Catholicism within the aboriginal populations varied considerably among tribal groups.[25]   Clergy, never numerous in the Southwest, became even scarcer after the suppression of the Jesuits in 1767 and the secularization of the missions in 1835.   Mexican independence followed by the conquest of 1848 completely ruptured what remained of the original alliance between Cross and Crown.   Henceforth Catholicism was a minority religion associated with an ethnic group regarded by the dominant "Anglo" society as inferior and backward.

Moreover, U.S. Catholicism has been very slow in building structural bridges to the Hispanic population.[26]   Until about 1970, despite ever greater numbers, Mexican Americans were nearly voiceless in their Church at all levels.   One historian, Moíses Sandoval, put the situation this way:

> Although in absolute numbers the Hispanic population increased in the last half of the nineteenth century, it had declined steadily as a proportion of the total population throughout the Southwest. This trend lent authority to the hypothesis that the Hispanic, like the Indian, was destined to disappear. The Church, accepting that view, acted accordingly. It gave first priority to the Anglo American and to the immigrants from Europe.[27]

Both the financial and the human resources of the Church were withheld from Hispanics well into the middle of this century, and even today this grievance has by no means been entirely redressed.

Theologian Allan Figueroa Deck calls attention to the fact that other ecclesial supports have also been missing.   Immigrants from Europe arriving in America generally found enclaves of their compatriots assisted by parishes designed for them and serving them in their native language.   These national parishes, often accompanied by parochial schools, played a huge role in the acculturation of the new arrivals to U.S. society through the vast array of religious and social services they provided.   Hispanics, however, who are often not even immigrants but long-time residents of U.S. soil, have generally not been given such national parishes of

---

25. The various syncretisms which resulted from the contact of Catholicism with different tribes form a fascinating study in inculturation. See Spicer, pp. 502-16. For description and analysis of the contemporary situations among native peoples, see the works of Carl F. Starkloff, esp.: "Religious Renewal in Native North America: The Contemporary Call to Mission," *Missiology* 13:1 (Jan. 1985) 81-101; "New Tribal Religious Movements in North America: A Contemporary Theological Horizon," *Toronto Journal of Theology* 2:2 (Fall 1986) 157-71; "A Different Gospel? Evangelization among `The People,'" *The Way* 34:4 (Oct. 1994) 293-303.

26. See, e.g., Isidro Lucas, *The Browning of America: The Hispanic Revolution in the American Church* (Chicago: Fides/Claretian, 1981); chap. 3, "A Church That Is Not There," pp. 37-54.

27. *On the Move: A History of the Hispanic Church in the United States* (Maryknoll, N.Y.: Orbis, 1990), p. 41.

their own.[28] Deck asserts that this remains the case today, even though the 1983 Code of Canon Law makes the erection of such parishes easier than ever by conferring upon local bishops an authority for them that previously resided in Rome. Of the importance of such communities, the author states:

> The lack of juridically sanctioned Hispanic parishes with strong pastors identified with their people is perhaps the single greatest reason for the ineffectiveness of our outreach to Hispanics.[29]

In addition, Deck debunks the claim that Hispanics are under-served because they were the first to arrive without their own native clergy. Italians, too, says the author, arrived without clergy in the beginning, yet their clout in Rome was sufficient to effect change in that situation.[30]

Sandoval, however, detects the beginnings of a new awareness around the turn of the century.[31] Some pastoral efforts among Mexican Americans began to be undertaken, especially in Texas, where they were often initiated by communities of women religious. More predominantly Hispanic dioceses were erected, including Corpus Christi (1912), El Paso (1914) and Amarillo (1927), and San Antonio was raised to an archdiocese (1928). A trickle of Hispanic clergy and religious began to appear.

Momentum for more profound changes in Church attitudes and practice was set in motion in the war year of 1944. Archbishop Robert Lucey of San Antonio convoked a seminar for the Spanish-speaking which drew some fifty delegates from several western and southwestern dioceses. Later in the same year a second seminar was held in Denver. At these meetings the Church's work with Hispanics received serious and sustained reflection for the first time.[32] One of the results was that many of the dioceses of the region began to set up Catholic Councils for the Spanish-speaking. The purpose of these bodies was partly spiritual in nature, addressing the urgent catechetical needs of Hispanics. But the councils also undertook to address corporal needs by sponsoring clinics and housing, and special services for migrant workers. Long-term goals to improve educational and economic opportunities and eliminate barriers of discrimination were adopted as

---

28. A. F. Deck, *The Second Wave: Hispanic Ministry and the Evangelization of Cultures* (N.Y.: Paulist, 1989), pp. 58-9; also A. F. Deck, "At the Crossroads: North American and Hispanic," in Roberto S. Goizueta, ed., *We Are a People! Initiatives in Hispanic American Theology* (Minneapolis: Fortress, 1992), pp. 12-4.

29. Deck, "At the Crossroads," p. 13.

30. Deck, "At the Crossroads," p. 9.

31. *On the Move*, p. 41. On the early 20th-century history of Mexican Americans' relationship with the Catholic Church, see Jay P. Dolan and Gilberto M. Hinojosa, eds., *Mexican Americans and the Catholic Church: 1900-1965* (Notre Dame: U. of Notre Dame Press, 1994).

32. Sandoval, *On the Move*, p. 46f.; also, Sandoval, "Church Structures for the Hispanics," in *Fronteras*, op. cit., p. 413.

well. This led to the Church's increasingly activist stance with regard to efforts to end violence against Hispanics, attempts to organize farmworkers and other laborers, and in the civil rights' struggles commencing in the 1950s and '60s. The annual Campaign for Human Development collection, begun in 1969, for example, has become an important source of funding for Mexican American self-help groups like the Industrial Areas Foundation.[33]

Gradually councils for the Spanish-speaking began to appear in other parts of the country where Hispanics concentrated. The Second Vatican Council gave a great boost to local efforts and to a broader change of consciousness. The postconciliar years also saw the formation of *PADRES*, an organization of Hispanic clergy, and *Las Hermanas*, Hispanic women religious, both of which played strong advocacy roles for their people. Increasingly, also, pastoral endeavors were coming to be organized and coordinated on regional and national levels. The Midwest Hispanic Catholic Commission, for example, which serves Hispanics in eight states from South Bend, Indiana, dates from 1965.[34] Seven such regional offices exist today.

The most influential of the regional offices, however, has been and continues to be the Mexican American Cultural Center (MACC), founded in 1971 in San Antonio under the able leadership of Father Virgilio Elizondo.[35] MACC has become well-known as a center not only of language studies but of liturgical, pastoral and theological inculturation. It owes much of its vitality and financial viability to Patricio Flores. Flores' ordination as the first Hispanic bishop in the U.S. in 1970 was an event of considerable symbolic weight for Hispanics and especially for Mexican Americans. Himself a child of an impoverished south Texas family, Flores became known as a defender of the poor, including the undocumented. He was named archbishop of San Antonio in 1979, a position he holds to this day.

Hispanic concerns have gradually found a place within the national bureaucracy of the Church as well. The 1944 seminar in San Antonio had resulted in a regional standing bishops' committee for the Spanish-speaking. Assuming national responsibility in 1964, it was finally placed under Hispanic leadership in 1967. The office moved to Washington in 1971 in the reorganization of the United States Catholic Conference. In 1974 its status was elevated to secretariat, the highest departmental rank. The Secretariat for Hispanic Affairs played a key role

---

33. Acuña, pp. 430-7.
34. Sandoval, "Church Structures...," p. 420.
35. Sandoval, "Church Structures...," pp. 431-4.

in the evolution of the *National Pastoral Plan for Hispanic Ministry*, as we shall see, and it continues today in a critical advisory role to the bishops.[36]

Despite the progress made in recent decades, however, Hispanics continue to be seriously under-represented in Church decision-making. By the early 1990s Hispanics comprised more than one third of the total U.S. Catholic population. However, out of a total of 402 Catholic bishops in the U.S., only 20 (5%) were Hispanic in 1993.[37] Fewer than five percent of U.S. Catholic priests are Hispanic.[38] Contrast these figures with those for Catholics of Irish descent, who make up approximately 17% of the U.S. Church but nearly half of the hierarchy and more than one third of the clergy.[39]

Although institutional arrangements do shape people's lives in important ways, the religious life of people is of course lived out essentially in everyday life. The characteristics of popular piety and religious practice give us perhaps our most indispensable information regarding the cultural ethos of a people. Mexican Americans, and Hispanics generally, have traditionally enjoyed a colorful and richly diverse faith at the levels of the local community, the family and the individual. We turn now to an examination of that popular religiosity.

Presiding over this entire realm stands the serene Virgin of Guadalupe, patroness of Mexico. It would be difficult to overestimate the cultural significance of Guadalupe. "One cannot know, understand, or appreciate the Mexican people without a deep appreciation of Guadalupe."[40] In south Texas and the *barrios* of Los Angeles her image is nearly as ubiquitous as in Mexico City; she adorns churches, homes, roadsides, workplaces, busses. She has been invoked in moments of national calamity, in the Mexican War of Independence, in the Mexican Revolution and in Cesar Chavez' struggle to organize the farm workers of the Southwest. Her feastday, 12 December, stands at the head of the popular religious calendar and is celebrated with grand processions and *fiestas*. The shrine of Guadalupe on the outskirts of Mexico City draws throngs of pilgrims every day and seldom fails to impress visitors.

---

36. Sandoval, *On the Move*, p. 71, and "Church Structures...," pp. 426-8. On the development of Hispanic ministry in the U.S., see also María Teresa Gastón Witchger, "Recent History of Hispanic Ministry in the United States," in María Soledad Galerón et al., eds., *Prophetic Vision: Pastoral Reflections on the National Pastoral Plan for Hispanic Ministry* (Kansas City: Sheed & Ward, 1992), pp. 183-99.

37. Gilbert R. Cadena, "Religious Ethnic Identity: A Socio-Religious Portrait of Latinas and Latinos in the Catholic Church," in Anthony M. Stevens-Arroyo and Gilbert R. Cadena, eds., *Old Masks, New Faces: Religion and Latino Identities* (N.Y.: Bildner Center for Western Hemisphere Studies, 1995), p. 37.

38. Cadena, p. 37.

39. Ibid.

40. V. Elizondo, *The Future Is Mestizo*, p. 59. Allan Deck agrees: "The Guadalupe experience is central to any understanding of Mexican Catholicism today." [*The Second Wave*, p. 37.]

The story of Guadalupe does not require a detailed recounting here.[41] Central to that narrative is the apparition of Mary, the mother of Jesus, to a poor young *indio*, Juan Diego, in the year 1531 – just ten years after Cortez had forcibly subdued the Aztec empire. But this was no ordinary, European-looking Virgin Mary. The Virgin of Guadalupe was not Spanish but *morena*, brown-skinned, and she spoke Nahuatl, the native language. She appeared on the hill of Tepeyac, an ancient site of pilgrimage and sacrifice to the Aztec mother-goddess, Tonantzín.[42] She left behind, on Juan Diego's *tilma* (cloak), her exquisitely beautiful and highly symbolic image. Each element of this icon, still revered at Guadalupe today, contains particular significance in Aztec mythology and culture.[43] In the figure of the Lady many elements of indigenous culture were caught up, affirmed and transformed with Christian meaning.

But, as Elizondo says, "The real miracle [of Guadalupe] was not the apparition but what happened to the defeated Indian."[44] The indigenous people of central Mexico had seen their magnificent, ancient civilization abruptly destroyed by the Spaniards. They had been robbed of their lands and subjugated to Spanish taskmasters. Although their cult had been violently suppressed, evangelization of the conquered people had not met with much success in those first twelve years of intercultural contact.[45] In contrast, it is estimated that in the six years following the events at Tepeyac, there were nine million converts among the native peoples of Mexico,[46] and this despite considerable official Church opposition to the spread of the devotion. For Elizondo, the Guadalupe legend represents nothing less than the "resurrection" of an enslaved and dying people. He says:

> Guadalupe is not just an apparition, but a major intervention of God's liberating power in history.[47]

---

41. The focus of the present study is the mythic power of the Guadalupe cycle in the life of the Mexican American people. The historical basis of Guadalupe is another matter, and it is the subject of some scholarly dispute. For a review of the documentary sources of the Guadalupe narrative, see Jeanette Rodriguez, *Our Lady of Guadalupe: Faith and Empowerment among Mexican-American Women* (Austin: University of Texas Press, 1994), pp. 16-9.

42. V. Elizondo, *La Morenita: Evangelizer of the Americas* (San Antonio: Mexican American Cultural Center, 1980), pp. 72-3.

43. For a detailed explanation of the symbolic meanings at work within each aspect of the icon and drama of Guadalupe, see V. Elizondo, *La Morenita*, pp. 83-92.

44. *Galilean Journey*, p. 11.

45. *La Morenita*, pp. 47-56.

46. *La Morenita*, p. 97, citing Joseph Cassidy, *Mexico: Land of Mary's Wonders* (Patterson, N.J.: St. Anthony's Guild, 1958), p. 20. In *Galilean Journey*, p. 45, Elizondo gives an estimate of eight million in the first seven years.

47. *The Future Is Mestizo*, p. 59.

The power of hope offered by the drama of Guadalupe came from the fact that the unexpected good news of God's presence was offered to all by someone from whom nothing special was expected: the conquered Indian, the lowest of the low.[48]

Moreover, *La Virgencita* provides the very identity of a new, *mestizo* people. "Were it not for Our Lady of Guadalupe," the author says, "there would be no Mexican and no Mexican-American people today."[49] Explaining the enormously powerful impact of the Lady of Tepeyac upon the psyche and spirits of the native people, Elizondo concludes, "[Guadalupe] is the first real anthropological translation and proclamation of the gospel to the people of the Americas."[50] In sum, for Elizondo and doubtless for many others, Guadalupe has been nothing less than the very engine of inculturation for Mexican and Mexican American Catholicism.

Of course, Elizondo's enthusiasm for the cult of Guadalupe is not universally shared. Christine Way Skinner, for example, affirms the liberating potential of Guadalupe, but she does see Guadalupe as "ambiguous."[51] Skinner points out that Mexican society continues to endure enormous cleavages between rich and poor, *criollo* (white) and *indio*, men and women. In each case Guadalupe has at times been enlisted to reinforce a passive, even fatalistic stance not supportive of active struggle to eradicate injustice. A recent study of the relationship of Mexican American women to the myth of Guadalupe by theologian Jeanette Rodriguez confirms this ambivalent view. Rodriguez concluded that among Mexican American women Guadalupe functions as a powerful symbol of identity, of unconditional, nurturing divine love, and of the feminine, maternal aspects of the divine itself.[52] While admitting that the popular cult of the Virgin has contributed to keeping women in a subservient role, the author also concluded that as such women become more fully acquainted with the entire narrative and symbolism of Guadalupe, its liberatory and empowering aspects come more to the fore for them.[53]

Although the 12th of December has undisputed primacy, the Mexican American calendar of popular religion is punctuated by other feasts, too. Advent often includes the celebration of *Las Posadas*, the nine days before Christmas when various festivities are held in honor of the nine months Mary carried Jesus in the womb. The statues of Mary, Joseph and the donkey are carried from house to house seeking shelter. When they are finally admitted, a great party is held, which usually

---

48. *Galilean Journey*, p. 12.

49. *The Future Is Mestizo*, p. 59.

50. *The Future Is Mestizo*, p. 60. For more of Elizondo's reflections on Guadalupe, see *La Morenita*, esp. pp. 101-20; also his recent work, *Guadalupe: Mother of the New Creation* (Maryknoll, N.Y.: Orbis, 1997).

51. "The Phenomenon of Our Lady of Guadalupe in Mexico," *Mission* 2:1 (1995) 95-143, esp. 127-39.

52. Rodriguez, pp. 143-58.

53. Rodriguez, pp. 159-65. For a creative re-interpretation of Guadalupe from a liberationist perspective, see also Guerrero, *A Chicano Theology*, pp. 96-117 and 138-48.

includes *piñatas*. Blindfolded participants, usually children, strike at the *piñata* with a stick and try to break it open, spilling candy and gifts. *Las Posadas* climaxes with *Nochebuena*, the traditional Midnight Mass of Christmas, which is followed by a late-night *fiesta*.[54]

One of the principal days of the calendar is *Miércoles de ceniza*, Ash Wednesday, the first day of Lent. Churches expect huge crowds on this day as people come to be marked with the sign of the ashes, usually made from the burning of the palms from the previous year's Palm Sunday. For many Mexican Americans, reception of the ashes is regarded as more important than regular attendance at Mass or reception of the Eucharist. The tangibility of this sacramental, its connection with the land and its humble, penitential spirit hold deep appeal and express powerfully the relationship with God.[55]

Holy Week is both a solemn and a colorful time in Mexican American communities. The week begins with Palm Sunday, often marked with long processions accompanied by *mariachis*. Holy Thursday services frequently end with yet another procession, this one marking the journey to Gethsemane, and this is followed for many by a "holy hour" of silent devotion. Good Friday, however, is the high point of the week. Non-Hispanics may be startled by the vividness and emotionalism with which the crucifixion and death of Jesus are recalled. The *Via Dolorosa* is often quite literally reenacted. In some places the traditional Good Friday services are followed later in the day by *El Pésame a la Virgen*, the accompaniment of the Blessed Mother in her sorrow, and the *servicio del santo entierro*, the remembrance of the burial of Jesus. In Mexico and the Southwest it is not uncommon to also find within churches a shrine to the dead Christ. This fascination with death can also be observed at funerals and on *El Día de los Muertos*, All Souls' Day (2 November).[56]

Among the special moments of family life, three stand out as the object of special veneration among Mexican Americans. One is the celebration of the baptism of an infant. A peculiarly Hispanic aspect of this celebration is the importance ascribed to the relationship between the godparents (*los padrinos*) and the child, and between the godparents and the parents. This bond, called *compadrazgo*, is taken with the utmost seriousness. Another important day is the child's First Communion. Even very poor families outfit their youngsters in fine clothing, white shirt and tie for the boys, frilly white dress for the girls. A third sacred event is the *quinceañera*, the celebration of a girl's fifteenth birthday. This rite of passage generally includes attendance at Mass and the renewal of baptismal

---

54. V. Elizondo, *Christianity and Culture*, pp. 183-5; also, *Galilean Journey*, pp. 34-8.

55. V. Elizondo, *Christianity and Culture*, pp. 185f.; *Galilean Journey*, pp. 32-4; also, C. Gilbert Romero, *Hispanic Devotional Piety: Tracing the Biblical Roots* (Maryknoll, N.Y.: Orbis, 1991), pp. 57-70.

56. V. Elizondo, *Christianity and Culture*, pp. 186-9; *Galilean Journey*, pp. 41-3.

promises. All of these moments are marked by great *fiestas* according to, or even beyond, the family's economic means.[57]

Piety also features significantly in Mexican American home and family life. Commonly, houses are richly decorated with the distinctive, vivid style of Hispanic iconography. Many households contain an *altarcito*, or home altar. In a nook or corner of a main room, a statue of Mary or Jesus is prominently displayed, often accompanied by statues or pictures of other saints or loved ones, and further adorned with flowers, candles, or other decorations. The altar is the site of family rosary or other ritual devotions, especially prayers of petition and thanksgiving. A small, sacred space in the midst of the bustle of family life, the altar symbolizes the divine presence in the home.[58]

A final aspect of Mexican American popular religiosity to be mentioned here is the various spiritual associations and apostolic movements which have crossed the religious landscape. Historically Latin American Catholicism has been marked by a large number of lay religious confraternities, e.g., nocturnal adoration societies and Guadalupana associations. Since Vatican II these traditional *cofradías* have been joined by several new mass movements. Generally lay-led, these movements and associations often attract large numbers of Hispanics with their highly affective and strongly communal spiritualities.

Three such postconciliar movements are worth special mention. One that has had enormous influence among Hispanics generally, and also among English-speakers, is the *Cursillo de Cristiandad*, introduced from Spain in the 1960s. This "short course in Christianity" consists of an intensive weekend retreat and is geared toward conversion of the individual toward greater closeness with Christ and more generous service in the Church. "Unabashedly affective"[59] in character, the *Cursillo* continues to exercise a profound influence on many individuals, especially in virtue of its emphasis on lay leadership and faith witness.[60]

A second important movement among Mexican Americans is the charismatic renewal. Strongly biblical and christocentric, the renewal also emphasizes lay witness and belief in the miraculous power of the Holy Spirit both in the meeting and in everyday life. Deck explains its striking popularity among Mexican Americans in two ways. For one thing, he says, "The Hispanic people find [the charismatic renewal's] warmth and conviviality familiar – familiar to the popular religion they have left behind in Mexico."[61] Secondly, the author believes this movement, like the *Cursillo* and like the fundamentalist sects which have been

---

57. V. Elizondo, *Christianity and Culture*, pp. 190f.; re: the *quinceañera*, see also Romero, pp. 71-82.
58. Romero, pp. 83-97.
59. *The Second Wave*, p. 68.
60. *The Second Wave*, pp. 67-9; Sandoval, *On the Move*, pp. 84-5.
61. *The Second Wave*, p. 69.

growing rapidly among Hispanics, supplies an important sense of communal belonging, "the possibility of finding real fellowship."[62]

A third movement which has steadily gained in popularity and importance is the development of basic ecclesial communities (BECs). BECs were being formed in Brazil in the 1960s and soon thereafter in much of Latin America, including the U.S. Southwest. Affirmed by Paul VI in *Evangelii Nuntiandi* in 1975 and by the bishops of Latin America gathered at Puebla in 1979, the BECs began to receive official encouragement in the U.S. as well in the mid-1980s. Deck reports that there has been "a general conviction that the effective pastoral service of Hispanics must give priority to whatever process leads to the creation of viable small communities."[63] Small communities have grown rapidly among Hispanics in the U.S. as well, although they generally have not enjoyed the same level of official encouragement that they have received in Latin America.[64]

There is no doubt that these and other movements continue to play a crucially important role in the faith life of very many Roman Catholic Hispanics. Allan Figueroa Deck even says of their importance, "These movements have at times rivaled the parish as the basic unit or organizational force among Hispanic peoples in Mexico and the United States."[65] The movements have not only nourished the faith life of Hispanic Catholics, they have also served as crucial "schools of leadership," i.e., settings in which lay Hispanic leaders are recruited, trained and given responsibility.[66]

However, the movements have often been given an ambivalent reception by the institution. This may be due in part to the strong commitment to the parish which has marked the U.S. Catholic Church throughout its history. The parish structure, whatever its strengths, is not easily reconciled with the activities and interests of the free-standing movements. But, no doubt, the ambivalence is also due in part to cultural and linguistic prejudices. Bryan O. Walsh, one-time episcopal vicar for the Spanish-speaking, commented on the relationship of the movements to the official Church:

> Many of the difficulties but not all can be traced to what I would call a reluctant acceptance by the Church of cultural and language differences as a necessary evil during a limited period of adaptation.[67]

---

62. *The Second Wave*, p.70.
63. *The Second Wave*, p. 71.
64. Sandoval, *On the Move*, pp. 86-7.
65. *The Second Wave*, p. 63.
66. Edmundo Rodríguez, "The Hispanic Community and Church Movements: Schools of Leadership," in Dolan and Deck, eds., *Hispanic Catholic Culture in the U.S.*, pp. 206-39.
67. Quoted by Sandoval, *On the Move*, p. 87.

Popular religion has innumerable intricacies and subtleties, and so interpreting it in any given context is always a delicate task. Much of the current discussion about this complex subject lies beyond the horizon of the present project. In the preceding paragraphs I have followed the lead of Elizondo, Deck and others who approach the matter with a fundamentally sympathetic attitude. In this view the elements of popular religiosity are seen as expressing both group identity and, at times, protest or resistance.[68] Ricardo Ramírez, bishop of Las Cruces, New Mexico, summarizes this perspective. Ramírez admits that popular religion can produce

> ...fatalism whereby a person feels helpless in view of forces that control his life.... Popular religion can be utilized to keep a people down. Oppression can set in by making of religion a slave, a pacifier. The oppressed peoples can be convinced that God wills that they remain as they are.[69]

However, the author continues by identifying the positive aspects of popular religion as these:

> Popular religion provides answers and gives meaning to the gaps in human questioning.... Popular religion aids in the search for self-identity.... Popular religion can be a sign of resistance; it can be a political and social protest against the status quo.... For the people themselves popular religiosity can mean both a search for the true God and integral liberation and hope that their aspirations can and will be fulfilled.[70]

---

68. See, *inter alia*, V. Elizondo, "Popular Religion as Support of Identity: A Pastoral-Psychological Case-Study Based on the Mexican American Experience in the USA," in Norbert Greinacher and Norbert Mette, eds., *Popular Religion* (*Concilium*, vol. 186; Edinburgh: T. & T. Clark, 1986), pp. 36-43.

69. *Fiesta, Worship and Family* (San Antonio: Mexican American Cultural Center, 1981), p. 25.

70. *Fiesta, Worship and Family*, p. 26. The complex vitality of popular religion is finally beginning to receive the serious attention it deserves from the academy. In addition to the resources already mentioned, my perspective on popular religion has been influenced by the works of Orlando O. Espín, especially these articles: "Popular Catholicism among Latinos," in Dolan and Deck, eds., *Hispanic Catholic Culture in the U.S.*, pp. 308-59; "Popular Religion as an Epistemology (of Suffering)," *Journal of Hispanic/Latino Theology* 2:2 (Nov. 1994) 55-78; "Pentecostalism and Popular Catholicism: The Poor and *Traditio*," *Journal of Hispanic/Latino Theology* 3:2 (Nov. 1995) 14-43; "Tradition and Popular Religion: An Understanding of the *Sensus Fidelium*," in A. F. Deck, ed., *Frontiers of Hispanic Theology in the United States* (Maryknoll, N.Y.: Orbis, 1992), pp. 62-87. See also Michael R. Candelaria, *Popular Religion and Liberation: The Dilemma of Liberation Theology* (Albany: SUNY Press, 1990); Diego Irarrázaval, "Catolicismo popular en la teología de la liberación," in V. Elizondo et al., *Teología y Liberación: Religión, Cultura y Ética* (Lima: Instituto Bartolomé de las Casas, 1991), pp. 71-105; Arturo Pérez, *Popular Catholicism: A Hispanic Perspective* (Washington: Pastoral Press, 1988); Segundo Galilea, "The Theology of Liberation and the Place of 'Folk Religion,'" in Mircea Eliade and David Tracy, eds., *What Is Religion? An Inquiry for Christian Theology* (N.Y.: Seabury, 1980), pp. 40-45; Enrique Dussel, "Popular Religion as Oppression and Liberation: Hypotheses on Its Past and Present in Latin America," in Greinacher and Mette, pp. 82-94.

Thus, popular religion is neither to be dismissed nor to be accepted uncritically. In every case a theological evaluation of popular religiosity is only possible once its function in the life of a people is thoroughly studied and understood.

Deck emphasizes that the data of popular religion and culture are one of the two essential points of departure for any discussion of evangelization or pastoral planning for Mexican Americans.[71] The second is the larger socio-cultural situation in which Mexican Americans find themselves, i.e., the mostly urban and culturally Anglo environment of the U.S. We shall turn to the second shortly.

The foregoing sketch suggests a few summarizing remarks about the Mexican American religious situation in relation to pastoral planning efforts.

The religiosity native to Mexican Americans can be characterized as vivid, intensely affective, spontaneous, extroverted and demonstrative. It places a high value on the tangible, e.g., sacramentals, iconography and shrines. It is thus a deeply Catholic spirituality, insofar as it affirms the created order and enfleshes the sacramental principle. It is integrally rooted in the rhythms of family and home. It is strongly communal and participative in style, as one sees in the numerous processions, *fiestas* and movements.

At the end of the day, however, the relationship of Mexican American popular religiosity to ecclesial structures is equivocal. On the one hand, Mexican Americans are surprisingly loyal to a Roman Catholic identity, especially when one considers the long history of official bias and indifference. On the other hand, much of Mexican American popular religion often displays only a tenuous connection to the institution. The movements and devotions, for example, often tend to operate parallel to, outside of, or even in opposition to the parish. The image of Guadalupe captures much of the paradox which runs through Mexican American popular religion. Once rejected by the colonial Church, she now adorns most Mexican American churches. Later identified as the Mother of the Saviour, her cult has been officially embraced. But, for all that, she remains a curiously non-Roman, extra-hierarchical figure, at once affirming gift and prophetic challenge to the Church.

Thus, pastoral planning for Mexican American Catholics will have to deal with the contours of popular religion in ways that both affirm cultural identity and, at times, reinterpret or reshape that spirituality in the direction of liberation. Moreover, such planning will labor under the additional burden of having to overcome a history which has wrought many points of divergence and suspicion between the "official" and the "popular." The prospects for bridging that gap would appear to be uncertain, at best.[72]

---

71. *The Second Wave*, p. 117.
72. Robert E. Wright, "If It's Official, It Can't Be Popular? Reflections on Popular and Folk Religion," *Journal of Hispanic/Latino Theology* 1:3 (May 1994) 47-67.

Cultural Values

Both in its institutional affiliation and especially in its many popular manifestations, religion plays a tremendously important role in the life and culture of Mexican Americans. One cannot neatly separate the religious dimension from all other dimensions of Mexican American culture, for religious values suffuse these aspects of life as well. One can attempt, however, to identify and describe some of the other cultural values which characterize Mexican Americans, even as these values may be closely allied with the religious ones we have already explored.

La familia. Mexican Americans are a strongly family-oriented people. Family life provides not only the structures for meeting physical needs, but nurturance, convivial socialization and faith formation. Many pastoral ministers comment upon the centrality of family in Mexican American group identity, and upon the cohesiveness and durability of that family[73] even in the face of sometimes extremely difficult social and/or economic conditions in the U.S. I myself have witnessed the remarkable warmth of the Mexican American family and the tenacious loyalty to family by Mexican Americans on many occasions.

According to Elizondo, the Mexican American emphasis on family is closely linked with the value of **hospitality**.[74] Visitors, both kin and friends, are frequent in the home, and their needs are given a high priority. The tradition of hospitality helps to explain the fact that many Mexican American households shelter a large number of people, often including recent arrivals from Mexico. Moreover, although the nuclear family is the standard among Mexican Americans, they also retain a strong identification with the extended family. Both family loyalty and the habit of hospitality forbid turning immigrants away, however inconvenient or unexpected their presence may be. Elizondo notes that in this extended family structure particular respect is given to the *ancianos* (the elderly), especially the *abuelitos* (grandparents), who play a vital role in the bearing and transmission of tradition and culture. Typically, one might even say ideally, members of the extended family live in geographic proximity to one another in the same *barrio*.[75]

Loyalty to the family is closely allied with the Mexican American sense of *el honor*. It is not too strong, claims Ricardo Ramírez, to say that for Mexican Americans "an individual exists for the family, for its name and honor."[76] Fear of the consequences of tarnishing the family name plays a role in maintaining family unity.[77]

---

73. Ramírez, pp. 39-40; Elizondo, *Christianity and Culture*, pp. 158-64; Mario J. Paredes, ed., *The Hispanic Community, the Church and the Northeast Center for Hispanics* (N.Y.: Northeast Catholic Pastoral Center for Hispanics, 1982), p. 17.

74. *Christianity and Culture*, p. 159; Ramírez, p. 20.

75. *Christianity and Culture*, pp. 158-64.

76. Ramírez, p. 40.

77. Ramírez, p. 49.

Interestingly, however, neither Elizondo nor Ramírez makes mention of **machismo** as a cultural trait of Mexican Americans. The typecast aggressive, dominating Latino male has been extensively portrayed in the mainstream Anglo media. One Hispanic sociologist claims that *machismo* has been the object of very serious distortion both in the media and even in the treatment accorded it in most social scientific literature. This source admits that the Chicano family, like the family in most cultural groups, is male-dominated. But he rebuts the belief that the Hispanic self-understanding of *machismo* is necessarily pathological or violent. Indeed, he claims, the woman is typically accorded a distinct, elevated dignity in the family. On this view, the chivalrous *macho* as titular head bears and defends the whole family's identity and honor. In so doing he even serves to combat the assimilative and disintegrative forces of the dominant Anglo culture.[78] There can be little doubt that the Mexican American family is often experienced by women as oppressive. However, the link between *machismo* and preservation of Mexican American cultural identity is probably deserving of more attention and study than it generally receives.

Elizondo claims that Mexican Americans are heir to a culture which embraces a deep **sense of the tragic**.[79] The author traces this to the many collisions and conquests through which Mexican and Mexican American culture have been formed, and the acceptance of suffering and death as integral parts of the present life.[80] He contrasts this predisposition toward tragedy with the Anglo American sense of the epic, especially the epic narrative of the "self-made" individual heroically (and stoically) battling long odds. For the Mexican and the Mexican American, says Elizondo, "to live is to suffer without allowing suffering to conquer life."[81] In contrast, the Anglo is geared more toward personal success measured in possessions. At its worst, of course, the Mexican American sense of the tragic can collapse into passivity and fatalism. But we would do better to regard passivity and fatalism as aberrations which have been unfairly used as warrant for a pejorative stereotype of the Mexican and Mexican American.

Elizondo also makes this assertion:

---

78. Alfredo Mirandé, *The Chicano Experience* (Notre Dame: U. of Notre Dame Press, 1985), pp. 146-81. For a more nuanced, if somewhat less flattering, description of *machismo*, see Earl Shorris, *Latinos: A Biography of the People* (N.Y.: Avon Books, 1992), esp. pp. 430-8. Another penetrating analysis of the Hispanic family, including its male-dominance patterns, is that of David T. Abalos, *Latinos in the United States: The Sacred and the Political* (Notre Dame: U. of Notre Dame Press, 1986), pp. 62-80.

79. *Christianity and Culture*, pp. 156-7; cf. also Nobel prize-winning author Octavio Paz, *The Labyrinth of Solitude* (N.Y.: Grove, 1961).

80. *Christianity and Culture*, p. 171.

81. *Christianity and Culture*, p. 157. Shorris sees this attitude summed up in the Spanish verb *aguantar*, "to bear, to endure, to stand, to tolerate, to put up with." [*Latinos*, p. 105.]

One of the fundamental characteristics of the Indo-Hispanic is that he is a humanist who places the primary importance in the person. Nothing is more important than the person, and he is recognized almost intuitively as existing in community.[82]

The **importance of the person** is one of the primary observations consistently made by Anglo pastoral workers who work among Mexican Americans. As Elizondo suggests, this sense of personalism is not the "Marlboro man" individualism of Anglos. It is a value placed upon the person as part of a group, upon personal relationships and upon time given over to the cultivation of those relationships. This value contrasts sharply with the Anglo stress on institutions, structures, efficiency and function. Catholic sociologist Joseph P. Fitzpatrick explains that this *personalismo* means a preference for "relating to persons rather than to organized patterns of behavior efficiently carried out."[83] The difference can be clearly seen in the approach to law, for example, as Elizondo observes.[84] For the Mexican American, law is an abstract ideal toward which one strives.

The person-centered quality of Mexican American culture leads Elizondo to some interesting reflections upon the nature of communication in the culture.[85] Because of the emphasis upon persons and relationships, Elizondo describes communication as slow, unfolding gradually. Communication is "not just words of information," but aims at sustaining relationship and building common experience. It is also often indirect, especially with regard to communicating a negative answer. Saying no directly is not an accepted norm in many situations, particularly if the questioner is regarded as of a higher station in life, e.g., a boss, a wealthy person, an elder, a priest or religious. Communication is "totalist," i.e., it attempts to grasp experience in its totality through not only words but emotions, gestures, sounds, actions. It is thus both rational and bodily rather than merely cerebral. Quite naturally, then, the Mexican American is very much at home in the world of symbol and ritual, and communication with regard to the mysterious or spiritual aspects of reality is not eschewed. All of these qualities can be readily observed in the public devotion of Mexican Americans to the graphic arts, music, poetry and dance.

Another cultural characteristic Elizondo points to is the **acceptance of the limitations of time**. The author laments the Anglo caricature of Mexican Americans as lazy. He claims that repetition of the word *"mañana"* ("tomorrow") has been misunderstood by outsiders. The Mexican American is a hard worker, says Elizondo, but is realistic about time and its limitations, and realistic about the possibilities of human accomplishment in time. The present has claims and joys

---

82. *Christianity and Culture*, p. 157; cf. also Paredes, p. 17-9.
83. *One Church, Many Cultures* (Kansas City: Sheed & Ward, 1987), p. 133.
84. *Christianity and Culture*, pp. 164-5.
85. *Christianity and Culture*, pp. 166-71.

and sorrows enough; pragmatic movement toward a future (e.g., retirement) is less important than today.[86]

Finally, Elizondo describes the robust Mexican American sense of *fiesta*.[87] Occasions of celebration punctuate daily life, church life, social life. Poignantly, however, Elizondo interprets the *fiesta* as an act of resistance and hope:

> The Latino does not party because things are going well, or because there are no problems or difficulties; he celebrates because he is alive. He celebrates because of his sense of the tragic, accepting the many different forces of life and yet realizing there is the ultimate happiness which has already begun. He does not allow himself to be swallowed up by the many tensions and problems, the moments of sickness and death that are part of life, but he rises above them and celebrates life. This is why the fiesta is such a symbol of the Latino world.[88]

There is more than meets the eye in the parties for which Mexican Americans are renowned. Love for life, deep faith, personalism, strength in the face of difficulty – all of these are reflected in the *fiesta*.

Pastoral Challenges

The U.S. Catholic Church has been slowly coming to recognize the pastoral crisis it faces in its Mexican American and other Hispanic members. The magnitude of the challenge can be approached in a preliminary way through consideration of a few basic demographic statistics.

The Hispanic population of the United States is large and it continues to grow rapidly, both in absolute numbers and relative to other racial and ethnic groups as well. According to government estimates, in 1995 there were approximately 26.8 million people of Hispanic origin in the United States.[89] This figure represents an 83.6% increase over the 1980 decennial census count of 14.6 million.[90] In 1980 the Hispanic population represented 6.4% of the total U.S. population; by 1995 that figure had risen to just under ten percent. It is estimated that there will be 31.2 million Hispanics by the year 2000,[91] and that sometime in the first half of the next

---

86. *Christianity and Culture*, pp. 171-2; Paredes, p. 17.

87. *Christianity and Culture*, pp. 172-3; Ramírez, pp. 21, 50-2.

88. *Christianity and Culture*, p. 172.

89. Louise L. Hornor, ed., *Hispanic Americans: Á Statistical Sourcebook* (Palo Alto, CA: Information Publications, 1995), p. 8. All statistics employed here are drawn from U.S. Federal Government sources, primarily the Bureau of the Census. U.S. government statistics are generally considered conservative in their counting of Hispanics and other urban minorities. One source, for example, cites the claim that the 1980 census may have undercounted Hispanics by as much as 7%. [Schick, below, p. 1] Another source estimates that between two and six million Hispanics were missed by the 1990 census. [Cadena, p. 55, n. 19]

90. Hornor, p. 3.

91. Hornor, p. 8.

century Hispanics will surpass African Americans as the nation's largest minority group.[92]

The Hispanic population is also quite young; median age among Hispanics in 1992 was 25.8 years, contrasted with 33.4 for the population as a whole.[93] Only 7% of Hispanics are over 60 years of age, while 17% of non-Hispanics are over 60.[94]

Although Hispanics are found in all fifty states, they are not distributed evenly. More than half of them live in either California or Texas; 88% live in the nine states of California, Texas, New York, Florida, Illinois, Arizona, Colorado, New Mexico and New Jersey.[95] Moreover, in contrast to their earlier agrarian roots, they are an urban people, indeed more urbanized than any other U.S. population group except Asians. 88% of Hispanics live in cities, and 58% of urban Hispanics live in the inner cities.[96] Not surprisingly, then, we find that crime victimization rates among Hispanics are higher than among white Americans (100.1 per 1000, vs. 88.7 per 1000).[97]

Within the Hispanic population, people of Mexican origin (which includes a spectrum from those newly arrived from Mexico all the way to those whose family roots in the Southwest predate 1848) are the most numerous group by far. Those of Mexican origin are about 62% of all Hispanics; the next largest cohorts are Puerto Ricans (13%) and Cubans (5%).[98] The Puerto Ricans are generally concentrated in New York and New Jersey, the Cubans in south Florida.[99] The Mexican-origin growth rate of 54.4% during the decade of the 1980s, although less than the rate for some Asian groups (Chinese, Filipinos, Asian Indians, Koreans and Vietnamese), made them the fastest-growing Hispanic group.[100]

Hispanics, Mexican Americans among them, continue to face serious economic disadvantages. The 1993 civilian unemployment rate was 10.6% among Hispanics, 6.0% among whites, 6.8% overall.[101] Per capita income among Hispanics in 1992 stood at $8,874, well off the overall U.S. average of $15,033.[102] By some measures conditions for Hispanics have been worsening. Over the period from 1980 to 1992, median family income among all Hispanics fell from $25,087

92. Marlita A. Reddy, ed., *Statistical Record of Hispanic Americans* (Detroit: Gale Research Inc., 1993), p. 190.

93. Hornor, p. 3.

94. Frank L. Schick and Renee Schick, eds., *Statistical Handbook on U.S. Hispanics* (Phoenix: Oryx Press, 1991), p. 2.

95. Schick, p. 8 (1989 figure).

96. Deck, *The Second Wave*, p. 11; Schick, p. 2.

97. Hornor, p. 189.

98. Schick, p. 7.

99. Deck, *The Second Wave*, p. 10f.

100. Reddy, p. 185.

101. Hornor, p. 131.

102. Hornor, p. 171; all figures in US dollars.

to $23,901 when adjusted for inflation.[103] The percentage of Hispanics below the government's statistical poverty line climbed over the same period from 25.7 to 29.3; among the population as a whole it rose from 13.0% to 14.5%.[104] The poverty rate among Hispanic children rose from one third to nearly four in ten, almost twice the national rate.[105] In breakdowns of these economic figures among Hispanic groups, Mexicans generally fare slightly better than Puerto Ricans but lag far behind Cubans. For example, 1992 median family income among Mexicans was $23,714, among Puerto Ricans $20,301 and among Cubans $31,015.[106]

Educational figures paint a similar picture. Although high school dropout rates among Hispanics have been falling, they remain about 150% the rate among whites.[107] While the high school completion rate among whites rose from 1975 to 1989, approaching 90%, the rate among all Hispanics leveled off below 60%.[108] 1990 figures show that 21.9% of the total U.S. population had completed an undergraduate degree; this included 22.6% of whites, 9.0% of all Hispanics. Among those of Mexican origin the figure was even more dismal: only 5.4% had completed college or university, compared with 9.7% among Puerto Ricans and 20.2% among Cubans.[109]

Hispanics have become not only more numerous but more visible in a variety of professions and more influential in the political sphere. Prior to the 1994 elections, for example, the number of Hispanic elected officials had been increasing steadily.[110] Meanwhile, however, figures show that both the percentage of Hispanics registered to vote, and the percentage actually voting, declined significantly from 1972 to 1992.[111]

Based on the above figures, we can estimate that there are at least 17 million Mexican Americans in the United States. A median estimate is that 80% of Mexican Americans are baptized Roman Catholics, or 13.6 million.[112] A majority of all Catholics in California, Texas, Arizona and New Mexico are Hispanics; in the populous Archdiocese of Los Angeles the figure exceeds 70%. Hispanics are now the largest ethnic group within the U.S. Catholic Church. It is estimated that in 1980 28% of all U.S. Catholics were Hispanic; by 1990 they had grown to 35% of

---

103. Hornor, p. 154 (1992 dollars).
104. Hornor, p. 178.
105. Hornor, p. 179.
106. Hornor, p. 161.
107. Hornor, p. 69.
108. Hornor, p. 68.
109. Hornor, pp. 90-1.
110. Hornor, p. 97.
111. Hornor, p. 98.
112. Deck, *The Second Wave*, p. 12. Estimates as to the percentage of Mexican Americans who identify themselves as Catholic range as high as 90%+. On the other hand, a study reviewed by Andrew Greeley suggests that the figure could be as low as 71% and falling: "Defection among Hispanics," *America* 159:3 (July 30, 1988) 61-2.

the total.[113] If present trends continue, early in the 21st century Hispanics will comprise a majority of the total U.S. Catholic population.[114] Catholics comprise about one fourth of the total U.S. population, a figure that has held fairly constant over the last 50 years. While the number of Euroamerican Catholics continues to decline, high Hispanic fertility and immigration make up the loss.[115]

Allan Figueroa Deck suggests that it is pastorally useful to understand the various histories, intentions and social situations at work within the Mexican American population. In addition to those native-born to the U.S., he sees three different typologies of immigrants. The first is the short-term immigrant, mostly male and mostly undocumented, who comes to the U.S. seeking work, stays three months or less and then returns to Mexico. A second group, the cyclical immigrant, also comes without family, stays longer, but returns to Mexico on a regular basis. Thirdly there are the permanent immigrants, generally families who cross the border, often legally, intending to remain in the U.S.[116] Obviously the church-related interests and needs of these different groups of people may vary widely.

Deck states that the patterns of Mexican immigration to the United States differ from earlier immigrant groups in at least two important ways. One is that the Southwest U.S., the destination of choice for most of the new immigrants, already has an historically well-established Mexican population and association with the Spanish language, Catholic faith and Mexican culture. The other is the highly mobile character of the short-term and cyclical immigrants.[117] Moreover, the most recent Hispanic immigrants are entering the country at a time when cultural pluralism and toleration are more accepted features of U.S. society than was often the case for earlier immigrants.[118] Minority rights are enshrined in civil rights laws, for example, and bilingual education is available in many places. In spite of this, however, Deck claims that the homogenization of ethnic groups continues to be a powerful force in American society: "The data indicates that assimilation continues to be the long-term pattern."[119] In short, the Mexican American community finds itself in the throes of a struggle to come to terms with the often subtle assimilative pressures, to find a place within U.S. society while retaining its distinctive cultural identity and ethos.

---

113. Cadena, p. 36. The estimate was made by Ron Cruz, director of the NCCB/USCC Secretariat for Hispanic Affairs in Washington. [Cadena, p. 55, n. 19]

114. Deck, *The Second Wave*, p. 12.

115. Cadena, p. 48. For more on the social situation of Hispanics in the U.S., see Joan Moore, "The Social Fabric of the Hispanic Community since 1965," in Dolan and Deck, eds., *Hispanic Catholic Culture in the U.S.*, pp. 6-49; esp. pp. 11-20 on the Mexican American community.

116. Deck, *The Second Wave*, pp. 12-7.

117. Deck, *The Second Wave*, pp. 18-9.

118. Deck, *The Second Wave*, p. 19.

119. Ibid.

As we saw previously, Deck claims that the ethnic or national parish was a largely successful strategy employed by the American Catholic Church for dealing with earlier waves of immigrants. Although *de facto* national parishes remain common, due to the fact that Hispanics tend to congregate in their own *barrios* or neighborhoods, Deck is dismayed that the national parish was abandoned as a strategy just when it would seem to have been most needed by the large number of Hispanic immigrants since World War II. He concludes,

> The Hispanic community was to some extent deprived of the strong local institutional base that national parishes provided for generations of Catholic ethnics. The policy of trying to integrate the people of whatever ethnic background and language in a territorial parish promoted unity when it succeeded, but also deprived the less assimilated, less influential group (in this case, Hispanics) of the security and clarity that comes from having one's own turf.[120]

Deck even questions whether the contemporary promotion of multiculturalism in the Church only functions as "an excuse to close more churches" or an excuse to ignore specific cultural contexts within the typically large U.S. parish.[121]

Paired with this withering of the national parish Deck places the continuing dearth of Hispanic clergy. The author traces this, in part, to an historic condition in Mexico and all of Latin America. But he also sees it as emblematic of the Hispanic struggle within the U.S. church: Hispanic vocations have not been vigorously recruited, and the existing Hispanic clergy have often faced tensions and difficulties within an Anglo-dominated presbyterate and hierarchy.[122]

With few of their own in the clergy, few among the Anglo clergy who understand Hispanic culture or who speak Spanish, few parishes to serve them, in an era marked by an overall contraction of both human and financial resources, the institutional base for serving Hispanic people remains weak. True, there are a few bright spots in the current picture. Among them Deck notes the proliferation of Spanish-language catechetical and leadership formation programs,[123] the staunch public defense of the undocumented given in recent years by the U.S. bishops, and

---

120. Deck, *The Second Wave*, p. 59. On the role of national parishes in buffering immigrant groups to the U.S. from the pressures of cultural assimilation, see Joseph P. Fitzpatrick, *One Church, Many Cultures: The Challenge of Diversity* (Kansas City: Sheed & Ward, 1987), pp. 103-11. Fitzpatrick fundamentally agrees with Deck's assessment that the absence of national parishes is a critical liability for Hispanics. [*One Church, Many Cultures*, p. 156]

For a brief overview of the history of national parishes in the U.S. Catholic Church, see Jay P. Dolan, *The American Catholic Experience* (Garden City, N.Y.: Doubleday, 1985), esp. pp. 158-220. More extended treatment can be found in Dolan's two-volume *The American Catholic Parish: A History from 1850 to the Present* (N.Y.: Paulist, 1987).

121. "The Crisis of Hispanic Ministry: Multiculturalism as an Ideology," 35.

122. Deck, *The Second Wave*, pp. 59-60.

123. Deck, *The Second Wave*, pp. 75-8.

the work on behalf of both legal and illegal immigrants rendered by Catholic agencies.[124] But very many pastoral needs among Hispanics still go unnoticed or unattended. Hispanics are seldom made to feel welcome or invited to ownership of their Church. Worse yet, too often, intentional or not, "the promotion of assimilation or Americanization is put before evangelization."[125]

But others are quite eager to fill the pastoral gap and engage in an energetic proselytization of Hispanics. Evangelical, fundamentalist and pentecostal Christian churches, and various sectarian movements are growing rapidly among Hispanics, especially Mexican Americans. In any Hispanic *barrio* these days one can observe the burgeoning number of storefront churches. Andrew Greeley estimates that a million Hispanics left the Catholic Church from 1973 to 1988, three fourths of them to become Baptist or fundamentalist.[126] Another source claims that the number of Protestant Hispanic pastors, seminarians and other religious leaders is now far greater than the number of their Catholic counterparts.[127] Greeley terms the attrition phenomenon "an ecclesiastical failure of unprecedented proportions."[128]

While some official hand-wringing over the hemorrhage has begun, deeper appraisal of the reasons for the shift is needed. Greeley sees the phenomenon, in part, as an aspect of the upward mobility of a new Hispanic middle class seeking respectability in American society.[129] But Greeley's analysis would seem to address only the outermost layer of the phenomenon. Elizondo offers a more penetrating analysis. He notes that, on the one hand, Protestant fundamentalism is often accompanied by a certain iconoclasm with regard to the images and practices of Hispanic popular piety.[130] Thus the shift from Catholicism to fundamentalism can result in a certain amount of violence done to Hispanic culture. On the other hand, he says, the embrace of fundamentalism is often experienced as "a great experience of liberation" in that it frees Hispanics "from the tutelage and control of foreigners" they must endure in Roman Catholicism.[131]

Allan Deck, for his part, has repeatedly tried to sound the alarm about the departure of large numbers of Hispanics from the Catholic fold.[132] Deck attributes the departure of Hispanics for other churches to three factors: 1) the dearth of

124. Deck, *The Second Wave*, pp. 83-7.
125. Deck, *The Second Wave*, p. 61.
126. "Defection among Hispanics," p. 61.
127. Cadena, p. 49.
128. "Defection among Hispanics," p. 62.
129. Ibid.
130. "Hispanic Theology and Popular Piety," 9-10.
131. "Hispanic Theology and Popular Piety," 10.
132. *The Second Wave*, pp. 138-41; "The Challenge of Evangelical/ Pentecostal Christianity to Hispanic Catholicism in the United States" (Unpublished lecture, Cushwa Center for the Study of American Catholicism, University of Notre Dame, 1992); "Fundamentalism and the Hispanic Catholic," *America* 152 (Jan. 26, 1985) 64-6; "Proselytism and Hispanic Catholics: How Long Can We Cry Wolf?" *America* 159 (Dec. 10, 1988) 485-90.

Catholic ministers who speak Spanish and who respect Hispanics' cultural values; 2) the lack of "small, receptive, faith-sharing community contexts"; and 3) the absence of a mission orientation in most U.S. Catholic parishes.[133] Moreover, Deck believes that there is an "unanalyzed affinity" between Hispanic popular Catholicism and evangelical and pentecostal forms of Christianity.[134] Deck describes Hispanic piety as

> ...captivating and graphic, dramatic and emotive. It eschews the cognitive in its effort to appeal to the senses and the feelings.... Its main qualities are a concern for an immediate experience of God, a strong orientation toward the transcendent, an implicit belief in miracles, a practical orientation toward healing, and a tendency to personalize or individualize one's relationship with the divine.[135]

All of these cultural characteristics find a congenial home in evangelical and pentecostal churches. Deck takes a dim view of both mainline Protestantism and "normative Catholicism," and he concludes:

> The point I want to make here is that the movement from popular Catholicism to some form of evangelical or pentecostal Protestantism is not as strange and drastic as it may seem. In a certain sense the movement of Hispanics to evangelical religion is a way to maintain a continuity with their popular Catholic faith which in the period both before and after the Second Vatican Council has been disparaged, opposed, dismissed, or ignored by many official teachers of the Church.[136]

Deck protests that even in the postconciliar Church the efforts of theologians, pastoral agents and religious educators have too often been culturally uninformed, viewing "popular religiosity as a problem to be uprooted, not a strength upon which to build."[137]

Kenneth Davis, another theologian well versed in the Hispanic reality, concurs with Deck's estimation. Davis suggests that the cultural discontinuities involved in the transfer of affiliation are to some extent more apparent than real. In Davis' view, the emotionally charged climate and emphasis upon participation found in pentecostal churches, for example, is in large measure congruent with the culture and religiosity of Hispanics. In the longer view, Davis sees the shift as another manifestation of a protracted struggle between a lay-led system of popular religion

---

133. "The Crisis of Hispanic Ministry: Multiculturalism as an Ideology," *America* 163 (July 14-21, 1990) 34.
134. "The Challenge of Evangelical/Pentecostal Christianity to Hispanic Catholicism," in Jay P. Dolan and A. F. Deck, eds., *Hispanic Catholic Culture in the U.S.* (Notre Dame: U. of Notre Dame Press, 1994), p. 421.
135. "The Challenge of Evangelical/Pentecostal Christianity...," p. 422.
136. Ibid.
137. Ibid.

among the marginated on the one hand, and a rigid, standardized, official religion promoted since Trent on the other.[138]

Thus, the pastoral challenges facing the U.S. Catholic Church in its Hispanic component might appear to be overwhelming. The Hispanic population is large and growing rapidly. It is relatively young; youth and young families with children are abundantly in evidence in Hispanic neighborhoods and churches. It is a highly mobile, urban population. Hispanics, Mexican Americans in particular, are mired in poverty and not well served by the educational system. Hispanics struggle to overcome a history and present reality of prejudice and marginalization within U.S. society. They find themselves within a Church which does not understand their language, customs, or popular religiosity, a Church which in fact often does violence to their culture through subtle pressure to blend into the American melting pot. Despite the long and intimate association of Mexican culture with Roman Catholicism, some observers openly question whether Mexican Americans will remain much longer within a Church that seems institutionally so unresponsive to their needs and aspirations. Heading off a potentially disastrous future will be the most important task faced by the U.S. Catholic Church in the next century.

Surveying these daunting pastoral challenges, Jesuit sociologist Joseph P. Fitzpatrick concludes that Hispanic Catholicism in the U.S. faces a "current crisis of inculturation." The author continues:

> Hispanics are aware of the experience of European immigrants. Most of the descendants of European immigrants have lost the characteristics of the European culture from which they have come and have been absorbed into the dominant culture of the United States. This becomes the preoccupation of Hispanic religious and community leaders: will this happen to them? Will they become part of a homogeneous population of Americans or American Catholics as they lose the characteristics which give them a specific identity as a people and a specific identity as Catholics? Or will they be able to become an influential part of American life while still retaining their own cultural identity? Is this kind of cultural pluralism possible?[139]

---

138. Kenneth Davis, "The Hispanic Shift: Continuity Rather than Conversion?" *Journal of Hispanic/Latino Theology* 1:3 (May 1994) 68-79. Also, O. Espín, "Pentecostalism and Popular Catholicism: The Poor and *Traditio*," *Journal of Hispanic/Latino Theology* 3:2 (Nov. 1995) 14-43.

139. *One Church, Many Cultures*, pp. 125-6.

CHAPTER THREE

The *National Pastoral Plan for Hispanic Ministry*

Formulation of the Plan

The pastoral movement which would eventuate in the *National Pastoral Plan for Hispanic Ministry* began at a meeting in New York City in September of 1971. The director of the Hispanic Apostolate for the Archdiocese of New York, Father Robert Stern, invited some local leaders to a meeting with Father Edgard Beltrán. Beltrán had recently joined the staff of the United States Catholic Conference's Division for the Spanish-speaking. With the others, he was invited to discuss the possibility of forming a plan for Hispanic ministry in the region. In one of the discussions, Beltrán suggested the calling of a national *encuentro* (encounter, gathering, assembly) of Church leaders concerned with Hispanic ministry. The idea was received warmly. Soon, spearheaded by Pablo Sedillo of the Division for the Spanish-speaking, the proposal obtained the endorsement of Bishop Joseph L. Bernardin, the general secretary of the USCC.[1]

Edgard Beltrán also represented an important connection with the Church in Latin America. He had previously worked with the Latin American Episcopal Conference (CELAM), and had been involved with CELAM's 1968 assembly in Medellín, Colombia. It was the Medellín conference which set the Latin American Church decisively on a new course. Called to consider the coordinated implementation of Vatican II, the Medellín conference responded to the directive of *Gaudium et spes* to examine the "signs of the times" in the lived social reality of Latin America. In this method, as one participant observed, Medellín was "a great breakthrough."[2] Profoundly influenced by the work of educator Paulo Freire[3] and

---

1. "Genesis and Statement of Purpose of the Planning Committee for the First National Hispano Pastoral Encounter," from Planning Committee records, 1971-72, in Antonio M. Stevens-Arroyo, ed., *Prophets Denied Honor: An Anthology on the Hispanic Church in the United States* (Maryknoll, N.Y.: Orbis, 1980), pp. 181-2; also Sandoval, *On the Move*, p. 79, and "Church Structures for the Hispanics," pp. 428-9. Cf. also Robert L. Stern, "Evolution of Hispanic Ministry in the New York Archdiocese," in *Hispanics in New York: Religious, Cultural and Social Experiences*, vol. 2 (N.Y.: Office of Pastoral Research, Archdiocese of New York, 1982), pp. 283-366. On the history of Hispanic ministry in the U.S. up to and including the Encuentros, see also M. Sandoval, "The Organization of a Hispanic Church," in Dolan and Deck, eds., *Hispanic Catholic Culture in the U.S.*, pp. 131-65.

2. Archbishop Marcos McGrath, "The Impact of *Gaudium et spes*: Medellín, Puebla, and Pastoral Creativity," in Joseph Gremillion, ed., *The Church and Culture since Vatican II: The Experience of North and Latin America* (Notre Dame: U. of Notre Dame Press, 1985), p. 68.

3. Alfred Hennelly, *Theology for a Liberating Church* (Washington: Georgetown University Press, 1989), p. 72. Freire's best-known work is *Pedagogy of the Oppressed* (N.Y.: Seabury, 1973).

others, Medellín took a strong stand on behalf of social justice for the poor, and spoke approvingly of the growth of base communities.[4]

The theological and pastoral ferment which characterized the Latin American Church in the late 1960s and early '70s did not go unnoticed in the U.S.[5] The theology of liberation had burst onto the scene after the close of the Council. Gustavo Gutiérrez' seminal *Theology of Liberation*[6] made its first appearance in Spanish in the same year as the New York gathering. The planners of the First Encuentro in the U.S. were keenly aware of the developments taking place in Latin America. Following the bold lead of the bishops at Medellín, the planners stated that their goal was "to begin to develop a pastoral plan for the Hispanic American community"; to that end, they would "analyze the present pastoral situation in the Hispanic American community and discuss possible solutions to the many problems that exist."[7]

The planning group may have succeeded beyond their own expectations. Two hundred fifty people, mostly clergy and religious,[8] gathered in Washington in June of 1972. Considerable anger attached to a long list of historical grievances was expressed at the meeting. Many of the interventions urged the Church to move swiftly from a policy of assimilation to one of cultural pluralism.[9] Virgilio Elizondo, addressing the group, sized up the increasing Hispanic self-consciousness of their unique identity, and urged the delegates to strive toward a coordinated plan for addressing Hispanic pastoral needs.[10] Bishop Flores, who described the Hispanic situation as "desperate," recounted the bitter history of discrimination in the Church and called the Church to task for attitudes and structures that continued to exclude Hispanics.[11]

In the end, the First Encuentro issued a statement of 78 "conclusions," or demands.[12] Most of them were implicit in a principle articulated repeatedly at the

---

4. Hennelly, *Theology for a Liberating Church*, pp. 97, 83. The major documents of the Medellín conference can be found in English in Joseph Gremillion, ed., *The Gospel of Peace and Justice* (Maryknoll, N.Y.: Orbis, 1976), pp. 445-76. The complete texts, in English translation, were published as *The Church in the Present-Day Transformation of Latin America in the Light of the Council*, vol. 2, Conclusions (Washington: USCC, 1970).

5. Robert S. Pelton, *From Power to Communion* (Notre Dame: U. of Notre Dame Press, 1994). See also: Marina Herrera, "The Context and Development of Hispanic Ecclesial Leadership," in Dolan and Deck, eds., *Hispanic Catholic Culture in the U.S.*, pp. 166-205; Roberto S. Goizueta, "The Preferential Option for the Poor: The CELAM Documents and the NCCB Pastoral Letter on U.S. Hispanics as Sources for U.S. Hispanic Theology," *Journal of Hispanic/Latino Theology* 3:2 (Nov. 1995) 65-77.

6. *Teología de la liberación* (Lima: CEP, 1971); the first English edition appeared two years later (Maryknoll, N.Y.: Orbis).

7. "Statement of Purpose," Stevens-Arroyo, *Prophets Denied Honor*, p. 182.

8. Sandoval, *On the Move*, p. 82.

9. Sandoval, *On the Move*, pp. 79-81.

10. Stevens-Arroyo, *Prophets Denied Honor*, pp. 183-7.

11. Stevens-Arroyo, *Prophets Denied Honor*, pp. 187-95.

12. "Conclusiones: Primer Encuentro Nacional Hispano de Pastoral" (Washington: USCC, 1972).

gathering: "There must be greater participation of the Spanish speaking in leadership and decision-making roles at all levels within the American Church."[13] Some of the demands eventually were met in whole or in part, e.g., that the USCC office for Hispanics be elevated in stature, that more Hispanic bishops be named and that more regional pastoral offices for Hispanics be erected.[14] Others were flatly rejected: the fostering of base communities as a pastoral priority, the ordination of married men to the priesthood and of women to the diaconate, the inclusion of training in Spanish language and Hispanic culture in the formation of priesthood candidates in all dioceses.[15] Although Archbishop Furey of San Antonio remarked that the conclusions comprised a "Magna Carta" for Hispanic Catholics,[16] the demands of the Hispanic leaders received, on the whole, a tepid response from the bishops.[17]

Still, within the Hispanic community, the First Encuentro had generated a definite momentum and the process moved forward. In the wake of the national meeting a few regional and diocesan encuentros were held. Some of these proved to be angry and contentious, others less so.[18] In spite of their hesitations, the bishops approved a second national gathering.

The Second National Encuentro, convened in Washington in August 1977, was a significantly different affair than the first. The method of the first was basically "top-down," i.e., the bishops and a group of well-known Hispanic leaders brought together an elite gathering of Church professionals. By contrast, the laity played a much larger role in the Second Encuentro. The method used in the second began with a remarkably wide consultation of Hispanic Catholics in local communities. The aim of the planning group in this process was this:

> No one would take part in the Segundo Encuentro who had not first participated in a group "de base" in a small community. Achieving this would itself be a historic contribution of the Segundo Encuentro to the renewal of the Church in the whole world.[19]

---

13. "Conclusiones," Preface, p. 1.

14. "Conclusiones" #1, 5 (also 23), and 11, respectively; Sandoval, On the Move, p. 80f.

15. "Conclusiones" #19, 26, 39 and 46, respectively; Sandoval, On the Move, p. 81.

16. Sandoval, "Church Structures for the Hispanics," p. 429, citing an interview with P. Sedillo, June 1974.

17. See, e.g., the May 1973 report of the bishops' Ad Hoc Committee for the Spanish-speaking, responding to the conclusions of the First Encuentro; in Stevens-Arroyo, Prophets Denied Honor, pp. 201-7; Sandoval, On the Move, pp. 81-2.

18. Sandoval, On the Move, p. 81; Sandoval, "Church Structures for the Hispanics," p. 430.

19. María Luisa Gastón, ed., Proceedings of the II Encuentro Nacional Hispano de Pastoral (Washington: USCC, 1978), p. 65.

It is estimated that about 100,000 people joined in the process,[20] which sought to determine from the people themselves what their needs were and how those needs might be addressed by the Church. The fruits of this consultation were gathered at the diocesan level and channeled to the national meeting through working documents prepared by six regions. Five hundred delegates came to Washington, accompanied by another seven hundred observers. There was a significant youth representation and some of the delegates were even migrant farm laborers. A few bishops had attended the First Encuentro; thirty-four attended in 1977.[21]

The agenda of the Second National Encuentro consisted almost entirely of workshop discussions of various topics. The overall theme was evangelization, chosen in light of Paul VI's 1975 encyclical *Evangelii Nuntiandi*. Unlike the first meeting, the second was conducted completely in Spanish. Certainly the choice of language was a statement of Hispanic unity and identity.[22] However, it was felt by some that it gave an advantage to the more conservative Cubans and other recent immigrants, while diminishing the influence of Mexican Americans, many of whom were second-generation or more and more accustomed to English.[23]

There were forty-five conclusions in the final document of the Second Encuentro. Many of the goals of the First Encuentro were reiterated. The formation of base communities was reaffirmed as a high priority by the delegates.[24] Many of the conclusions outlined ways in which injustices both in the Church and society might be attacked.[25] Some observers, however, complained that the social and political analysis employed was weak and that parliamentary procedure muted the voice of the poor.[26] The assembly also gave strong support to lay ministries and lay formation efforts, especially among women and youth.[27] Moreover, the Second Encuentro offered a powerful vision of an evangelizing church based on collaborative ministry (*pastoral de conjunto*) and unity amid cultural pluralism.[28] While the tone of the statements which emerged in 1977 was somewhat milder than in 1972, it was nonetheless prophetic. More importantly, the Second Encuentro could more truly claim to be representative of the varieties of Hispanic experience and viewpoints. As one commentator said, "The *II Encuentro* recommendations

---

20. *Proceedings of the II Encuentro*, pp. 65-6.
21. Sandoval, *On the Move*, p. 82.
22. *Proceedings of the II Encuentro*, p. 66.
23. Sandoval, *On the Move*, p. 83.
24. *Proceedings of the II Encuentro*, pp. 68, 70.
25. *Proceedings of the II Encuentro*, pp. 71, 73-81.
26. Editorial, *Cara a Cara* 4 (Sept.-Oct. 1977); in Stevens-Arroyo, *Prophets Denied Honor*, pp. 325-6.
27. *Proceedings of the II Encuentro*, pp. 70-2, 76-9.
28. *Proceedings of the II Encuentro*, pp. 69, 82-3.

express the desire of grassroots Hispanics for a more responsive, multicultural, spiritually alive, united and creative Church."[29]

A few new initiatives followed the Second Encuentro. One was the formation of a National Youth Task Force (*Comité Nacional Hispano de Pastoral Juvenil*) to advise the Secretariat for Hispanic Affairs and the bishops on the needs of Hispanic youth.[30] More regional offices were opened and cooperation among them increased. The National Institute for Hispanic Liturgy, which has been an important resource for inculturation of the liturgy, was founded in 1979.[31] By 1988 the number of Hispanic bishops reached twenty. Spanish-language television programming and diocesan newspapers, almost non-existent before, became more common, especially in large urban areas.

Events in Latin America continued to command the attention of U.S. Hispanics and, to a lesser extent, the U.S. Catholic hierarchy. While much of Central and South America endured military dictatorship and civil upheaval, the bishops of CELAM convened again at Puebla, Mexico, in 1979. In spite of bitter feuding and the strenuous efforts of conservative prelates to derail the commitments made at Medellín, the Puebla conference reaffirmed the direction taken ten years earlier, especially the option for the poor.[32]

Prodded by the First and Second Encuentros and by the Latin American example at both Medellín and Puebla, the U.S. bishops responded in 1983 with a pastoral letter, *The Hispanic Presence: Challenge and Commitment.*[33] The letter was received with some disappointment in that it failed to forthrightly confess the history of bias and neglect which have so often characterized the Hispanic experience in the U.S. church. However, it did proceed from the perspective of respect for Hispanic culture, and it began with an honest appraisal of Hispanics' socioeconomic standing.

After applauding the recent achievements in Hispanic ministry, the bishops turned to the many urgent pastoral challenges the Church faced among Hispanics. They affirmed the *pastoral de conjunto* approach, adding: "Implicit in a *pastoral de conjunto* is the recognition that both the sense of the faithful and hierarchical

---

29. María Teresa Gastón Witchger, "Recent History of Hispanic Ministry in the United States," in Soledad Galerón et al., eds., *Prophetic Vision: Pastoral Reflections on the National Pastoral Plan for Hispanic Ministry* (Kansas City: Sheed & Ward, 1992), p. 192.

30. Witchger, p. 193.

31. Witchger, p. 193.

32. John Eagleson and Philip Scharper, eds., *Puebla and Beyond: Documentation and Commentary* (Maryknoll, N.Y.: Orbis, 1979); contains the Final Document of the conference (pp. 122-285), the addresses of Pope John Paul II and commentaries by Penny Lernoux, Moises Sandoval, Virgilio Elizondo, Archbishop Marcos McGrath, Jon Sobrino, Joseph Gremillion and Robert McAfee Brown.

33. National Conference of Catholic Bishops, *The Hispanic Presence: Challenge and Commitment* (Washington: USCC, 1983).

teaching are essential elements in the articulation of the faith."[34] They called for liturgy, preaching, catechesis, lay formation, schools and use of the media adapted to Hispanic culture. The bishops committed themselves to fostering Hispanic vocations to the priesthood and religious life, and admitted that the paucity of Hispanic clergy and religious owed in part to neglect and cultural conflict. They voiced objection to the "anti-Catholic spirit" found in the proselytizing of "Protestant sects" and "fundamentalist groups."[35]   Although affirming that ecumenical cooperation was important, they staked out Hispanics as Catholic turf:

> In the Hispanic context, however, the Catholic Church and its tradition has [sic] played the major historical role of inculturation of the Gospel; the Church is committed to continuing this mission.[36]

The bishops called for greater pastoral attention to Hispanic youth and families, and they objected strongly to the mistreatment of migrant farm laborers, especially the undocumented. Basing itself on the tradition of Catholic social teaching, the letter made a strong appeal for Hispanic civil rights and for the elimination of prejudice, racism and poverty.

The bishops also acknowledged the close link of U.S. Hispanics with Latin America and pledged their own continued interest and support of the Church there. They said:

> The Church in the United States has much to learn from the Latin American pastoral experience; it is fortunate to have in the Hispanic presence a precious human link to that experience.[37]

The bishops took a positive view of Hispanic popular religiosity, but they called for "a closer dialogue between popular and official practice."[38] In addition, the bishops spoke with surprising enthusiasm about the *comunidades eclesiales de base* springing up in Latin America and the U.S. Calling them "a ray of hope in dealing with dehumanizing conditions," and noting that they have brought "a revitalized sense of fellowship," the bishops concluded, "We highly encourage their development."[39] Significantly, in this section the bishops drew extensively on the

---

34. *The Hispanic Presence*, p. 13.
35. *The Hispanic Presence*, p. 19.
36. *The Hispanic Presence*, p. 20. This appears to be the only use of the word "inculturation" in the text.
37. *The Hispanic Presence*, p. 26.
38. *The Hispanic Presence*, p. 26.
39. *The Hispanic Presence*, p. 27.

document of Medellín. And they re-envisioned the U.S. parish as a "community of communities," a structure comprised of flourishing base communities.[40]

In concluding their letter, the U.S. bishops committed the Church to respond to Hispanic pastoral needs as part of a larger commitment to "catholicity" and "pluralism," and they called on their Catholic flock to embrace this vision of Church.[41] They asked all U.S. Catholics "to work not just for Hispanics but with them" in order to deepen the common "preferential option for the poor."[42] Admitting that the Church's present commitment of financial resources to Hispanic ministry was inadequate, the bishops committed themselves vaguely to change and further study. Finally, the bishops called for a Third Encuentro, whose process was to go forward "from *comunidades eclesiales de base* and parishes, to dioceses and regions, and to the national level."[43] The conclusions of this encuentro, the bishops promised, would serve as "a basis for drafting a National Pastoral Plan for Hispanic Ministry."[44]

Much of the bishops' pastoral letter might have been easily dismissed as well-intentioned, if belated, rhetoric. But the affirmation of the base communities and their explicit inclusion in a process leading into collaboration with the hierarchy in forming a national pastoral plan reverberated powerfully through the Hispanic community. Preparations began immediately for the Third Encuentro.

The consultation which led up to the next national meeting was astoundingly ambitious in scope. The bishops' Ad Hoc Committee for Hispanic Affairs had wisely proposed four objectives for the process: 1) that it be, in itself, an experience of evangelization; 2) that it call forth and form leadership; 3) that it develop from the grass-roots level; 4) that it strengthen the diocesan and regional meetings.[45] To accomplish these goals, and to achieve the end result of promulgating a pastoral plan, the process had to be carefully designed. (See diagram next page.)

The process began with formation of diocesan "promoter teams." Their task was to publicize and facilitate the consultation process at the local level, seeking the advice of the grass-roots folk as to the pastoral priorities which should be brought to the national meeting. One commentator calls the role of these promotion teams "the key to successful implementation of the design."[46] At the same time, "mobile teams" were formed to conduct a broad, door-to-door canvass of Hispanics who were alienated from the Church. In Miami alone, 11,000 households were said to

40. *The Hispanic Presence*, p. 27. The phrase has been attributed to Cardinal Joseph Bernardin.
41. *The Hispanic Presence*, pp. 29-30.
42. *The Hispanic Presence*, p. 30; the Puebla document is cited.
43. *The Hispanic Presence*, p. 32.
44. *The Hispanic Presence*, p. 32.
45. Pablo Sedillo, ed., *Prophetic Voices: The Document on the Process of the III Encuentro Nacional Hispano de Pastoral* (Washington: U.S. Catholic Conference, 1986) p. 5.
46. Witchger, p. 196.

III NATIONAL ENCUENTRO PROCESS

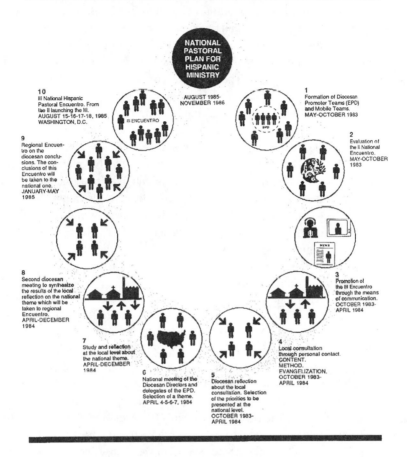

[Figure 2. From *Prophetic Voices*, p. 4.]

have been visited.[47] Following these efforts, many dioceses held their own encuentros to gather and unify the local input. In April of 1984 diocesan directors of Hispanic ministry (mostly clergy and religious) and representatives of the promoter teams (mostly lay) met to review the preliminary results of the consultation and to select a theme for the national assembly. Since the bishops, in convoking the Tercer Encuentro, had called on Hispanics to "raise their prophetic

47. Sandoval, *On the Move*, p. 83.

voices to us once again,"[48] the group chose the theme *"Pueblo Hispano: Voz Profética."*[49]

A second round of consultation then commenced. Base communities and parish groups engaged in study and response to the theme. These reflections were synthesized at diocesan meetings, which were in turn followed by regional encuentros. The regional meetings, large events in themselves, were held in the winter and spring of 1985. The regional conclusions were then sent to the Secretariat for Hispanic Affairs in Washington. That office edited them into a working document for the national encuentro.[50] In all, more than 200,000 people had taken part in a process stretching over some eighteen months.[51]

1,148 people, representing 134 dioceses, arrived at Catholic University in Washington for the Third Encuentro, 15-18 August 1985. The planners established formulas to ensure fair representation and participation by marginated groups, and the resulting identity of the delegates demonstrates that the quotas were largely successful. Fifty-six bishops and major superiors were in attendance, 168 priests, 125 religious and 799 laity. Slightly less than half of the participants were women, surpassing the minimum goal of 40%. About 13% of the attendees were youth, ages 18-25, falling short of the goal of 20%. 17% of the delegates were farm workers, laborers, or unemployed.[52]

The ethnic and regional balance of the assembly was similarly impressive, though not perfect. The Northeast region was home to 28% of the delegates, followed by 19% from the Midwest. Only about 20% of the delegates hailed from the Southwest, meaning this region was considerably under-represented. 78% of the attendees claimed U.S. citizenship, 17% said they were documented aliens, and two percent undocumented. About 41% of the participants identified themselves as either Mexican or Mexican American. Puerto Ricans made up 15%, Cubans 9% and South and Central Americans more than 11%. Although there appears to have been some difficulty in self-identification for those responding to the demographic survey (19% marked "Other"), the Mexican/Mexican American segment was probably under-represented by as much as 19%.[53]

The Third Encuentro also drew together an assembly of people with strong leadership credentials. 21% had attended the Second Encuentro in 1977. Over 90%

48. *The Hispanic Presence*, p. 32.

49. *Prophetic Voices*, p. 5.

50. Consuelo Tovar, ed., *Documento de Trabajo: III Encuentro Nacional Hispano de Pastoral,* Edición Bilingüe (Washington: U.S. Catholic Conference, 1985).

51. Deck, *The Second Wave*, p. 89.

52. *Prophetic Voices*, p. 5; and David S. Blanchard, "The *III Encuentro*: A Theological Reflection on a Classic Church Event," in Galerón et al., *Prophetic Vision*, pp. 204-5.

53. Blanchard, "The *III Encuentro*," pp. 205-6.

had actively participated in all phases of the consultation process, and an overwhelming majority were regularly active in their local church communities.[54]

The parliamentary procedure followed at the Second Encuentro had been found to be somewhat tedious and stiff. Planners of the Third Encuentro set out to improve the structure, hoping to maximize participation and the reaching of agreement on concrete proposals.[55] Brazilian priest José Marins, well-known for his pathbreaking work with base communities in Latin America, and for his mediation skills at Puebla in 1979, was enlisted to help facilitate the process.[56] Delegates were divided into five halls of 230 people each, then into groups of about 45 and sub-groups of twelve to fifteen. Work was coordinated by a system of secretaries reporting to a steering committee. In spite of the unwieldy numbers and the breathless pace of the schedule, the process aimed at the building of consensus, "which was reached in practically all the decisions."[57]

The Third Encuentro issued 68 conclusions. The first nine, called "Prophetic Pastoral Guidelines," provided the foundation upon which thirty-five more specific "Commitments" were built. The final twenty-four points, "The Follow-up," were intended to ensure the implementation of the Encuentro's conclusions.

The "Pastoral Guidelines," although very general, represent the assembly's broad consensus on Hispanic values and needs. They are worth quoting here:

> 1. We, as Hispanic people, choose the family in all its expressions as the core of our pastoral ministry.
> 2. We, as Hispanic people, make a preferential option for and in solidarity with the poor and marginalized.
> 3. We, as Hispanic people, make a preferential option for Hispanic youth so that they will participate at all levels of pastoral ministry.
> 4. We, as Hispanic people, want to develop and follow a *pastoral de conjunto* that responds to our reality.
> 5. We, as Hispanic people, want to follow the pastoral approach of an evangelizing and missionary Church.
> 6. We, as Hispanic people, want to follow the pastoral approach of promoting Hispanic leadership that is incarnated and committed.
> 7. We, as Hispanic people, want to follow a line of integral education sensitive to our cultural identity.
> 8. We, as Hispanic people, want to follow the line of a Church that promotes and exemplifies justice.

---

54. Blanchard, "The *III Encuentro*," pp. 206-8.
55. Witchger, p. 196f.
56. Sandoval, *On the Move*, p. 83.
57. *Prophetic Voices*, p. 5.

9. We, as Hispanic people, wish to follow an approach of valuing and promoting women, recognizing their equality and dignity and their role in the Church, the family, and society. [6]

The "Commitments" which followed were intended to "reflect a change from being objects to subjects in pastoral ministry and from being recipients to agents of pastoral action." [5] They were grouped into five areas. Discussions on the theme of "Evangelization" noted that

An evangelization incarnated in a given culture is essential for all peoples, but it is especially important for the Hispanic people in this country. The temptation to cultural assimilation is constantly present, and in many cases it ceases to be only a temptation and becomes reality. [7]

Analyzing their own reality, the delegates complained of the perception that the Church was "cold, without fraternal love or a communitarian dimension [and] without a missionary dimension." [7] They felt that Hispanics had received short shrift from the hierarchy, that there was a lack of planning and coordination among pastoral ministers and too few invitations to participation. The result they saw was that Hispanics did not "feel welcomed, accepted, or listened to in the Church." [7] They pleaded for more priests, religious, catechists and other ministers who understood their culture and more use of the media in Spanish. They claimed that the centrality of the family and the contributions of women, youth and agricultural laborers were often ignored.

To remedy this situation, the first strategy they proposed was to make creation of base communities a high priority. They said:

We, as Hispanic people, commit ourselves to create and maintain small ecclesial communities in order to foster and share the Christian gifts incarnated in the Hispanic culture, developing the ecclesial awareness of our people, promoting a Church that is prophetic, evangelizing, communitarian, and missionary; in order to attract those alienated and separated from the ecclesial structures; in order to continue catechesis in accordance with the needs of our people; and in order to encourage prayer and reflection, sharing our faith, customs, and material and spiritual resources. [8]

They sought a "more personal" style of evangelization "oriented toward the formation of small communities." [8] They asked for diocesan planning, in the spirit of *pastoral de conjunto*, that would take their culture seriously, and for more pastoral centers and offices with more authority and resources. The delegates pledged themselves to consciousness-raising about the mass media, to creation of more television and radio programming geared to Hispanic needs and interests, and to be themselves "authentic evangelizers." [8]

The following section focussed on "Integral Education," which was described as "a global formation in the economic, political, social, cultural, family, and church aspects of life." [8]   The assembly decried the "great shortage of educational resources and programs that are adequate and respectful of [Hispanic] cultural values." [9]   The Church was excoriated for "still lacking full awareness of her responsibility with the Hispanic people insofar as she does not provide enough help or denounce concrete and institutionalized injustices." [9]   The delegates longed for more Hispanic clergy "as a defense against assimilation and a remedy for the lack of integral education," and for more centers for the work of evangelization and lay formation. [9]   In turn, they committed themselves to the development of integral education programs that would give priority to the family, to CEBs, to youth, to women and to the poor and marginalized.   Additionally, they pledged to work for raised awareness of cultural factors among pastoral leaders, for educational centers and mobile teams, for increased use of the mass media and for greater involvement in both the public and Catholic school systems.

Turning to "Social Justice," the Third Encuentro condemned a long list of injustices in U.S. society, in the Church and in U.S. relations with Latin America. The assembly committed themselves to continue to denounce violence, the arms race and other injustices, and to continue to work for human rights, especially the rights of workers, refugees and immigrants. Within the Church, they pledged "to work so that the Church may set an example in practicing her own social doctrine." [11]   They also demanded "the renewal of the traditional parish in order that it be open and effectively multicultural." [11]   Perhaps understandably, this section was short on specific actions to be taken.

The conditions of Hispanic youth received considerable attention from the encuentro.   The pastoral needs in this area seemed particularly pressing and intractable: while more than half of the Hispanic population is youth, "99% [of youth] are estranged from the Church." [11]   The delegates reviewed a litany of problems with drugs, violence, schools, materialism, cultural adjustment, etc., and noted sadly that the Church is doing far too little to help. Still, they looked to their youth to be "bridges between the Hispanic and the North American cultures, thus integrating the good from both cultures." [12]   The commitments which followed, however, were somewhat nebulous: creation of a national office, greater efforts and more programs at the local and diocesan levels and work for change in school systems.   No mention was made of youth involvement in CEBs.

In the final area, "Leadership Formation," the Third Encuentro asserted that Hispanics very much want to participate in leadership in church and society, but generally find themselves "far from the centers" of both. [13]   The assembly rued the dearth of both ordained and lay Hispanic leadership, mentioning the leadership needs of the CEBs in particular.   It felt that the inadequate education of the leadership that does exist served to "keep [Hispanics] marginalized in the face of the dominant culture." [14] The delegates committed themselves "to discover, motivate, support, promote, and foster leaders who come from the people, know the people, and live with the people." [14] They pledged to continue to seek ways to participate in decision-making, to bring leadership programs where they were needed most, to promote vocations to the priesthood, diaconate, religious life and lay ministries, to foster a collaborative style of leadership, and to raise social consciousness through civic outreach.

In terms of the follow-up, the first conclusion was to maintain the diocesan promotion teams which had played such a key role in the consultation process of the Third Encuentro. Calling for the development of diocesan pastoral plans based on the Encuentro conclusions, the delegates urged the teams and regional offices to publicize and direct the implementation of the plans. In particular, the delegates repeated their strong appeal for the formation of CEBs. They committed themselves to "take the process to the grass roots again" by sharing their experience of the Third Encuentro and its conclusions upon returning home. [15] They asked dioceses and parishes to oversee the launching of a vast though hazily defined evangelization project for the unchurched, a project which was to be directed toward integrating newcomers into small communities. The National Secretariat for Hispanic Affairs was requested to direct publicity, to conduct an evaluation of the Third Encuentro three years hence, and to organize future national assemblies every five years. The assembly closed with an appeal to the bishops for leadership and collaboration in implementing the conclusions on all levels.

Review of the Plan

After the close of the Tercer Encuentro, it took the U.S. bishops more than two years to write and promulgate the *National Pastoral Plan for Hispanic Ministry*. The Secretariat for Hispanic Affairs, directed by Pablo Sedillo, brought the results of the encuentro to the bishops and facilitated work on the Plan. A writing committee was appointed, chaired by Fr. Mario Vizcaíno of Miami.[58] The writing committee worked closely with the drafting subcommittee of the bishops' Ad Hoc Committee for Hispanic Affairs.[59] Numerous drafts and amendments were

---

58. Other members of the writing committee were Sr. Dolorita Martinez, Sr. Dominga Zapata, Rev. Ricardo Chaney, Sr. Soledad Galerón, Rev. Juan Díaz Vilar and Rosalva Castañeda; consultants were Rev. José Maríns, Sr. Teo Trevisan, Sr. Carolee Chanona, Maria Luisa Gaston, Rev. Domingo Rodriguez and Rev. Sabine Griego. [Source: a letter from V. Lopez to the participants, dated 31 Oct. 1985, shown to me by Mario Vizcaíno in an interview at the South East Pastoral Institute, Miami, 3 Jan. 1996.]

59. The drafting subcommittee consisted of Bishops Ricardo Ramírez, chair, and Peter Rosazza, and Archbishops Roberto Sanchez and Roger Mahoney. [Source: Abp. Sanchez, in a video of the presentation and debate of the NPPHM by the NCCB at their Nov. 1987 meeting, produced by the South East Pastoral Institute, Miami.]

produced over this period of months. Sedillo's assistant, Fr. Vicente Lopez, who served as secretary to the writing committee, played a crucial role, in part because of Sedillo's ill health over much of this time period.

Clearly among the bishops there were some hesitations about the encuentro process and the construction of a plan, though the project also had some important supporters. In presenting the plan to the bishops, Archbishop Roberto Sanchez of Santa Fe, New Mexico, addressed the comments and questions of bishops submitted during the process. These submissions revealed confusion and reservations in four areas. The first had to do with the precise nature of the plan in its relation to diocesan and regional structures. Sanchez responded that no diocesan prerogatives were being challenged and that the manner of implementing the plan would be left to the discretion of local bishops. The second area had to do with the stated purpose of integrating Hispanic Catholics into the life of the Church. Sanchez replied that Hispanics sought full participation in the Church. He stressed that Hispanics wanted to avoid being swallowed up by the dominant Anglo culture of the U.S. Church. However, while preserving their identity and culture, they did not want isolation, either. A third area of concern was the priority given to the encouragement of small communities. Sanchez emphasized that the communities were to be linked firmly to the existing parish structure. Fourthly, there was the matter of finances. Sanchez explained that the committee had avoided putting a price tag on the implementation but preferred instead to see the plan effected through existing structures and processes.[60]

Whatever their misgivings, the bishops unanimously promulgated the Plan we now have at their November 1987 meeting in Washington. It is a concise document, the English text running a mere twenty-nine pages. Although the Plan was written in response to the pastoral needs of Hispanics, it was "addressed to the entire Church in the United States.... challenging all Catholics as members of the Body of Christ." [#1] The bishops acknowledged their debt to the Hispanic people themselves, calling the Plan "the result of years of work involving thousands of people who participated in the III Encuentro [and] a strategic elaboration based on the conclusions of that Encuentro." [#1] Additionally they prefaced the document with "a sense of urgency," at the same time cautioning that it must be implemented "with due regard for local adaptation." [#2]

The "Introduction" set forth the goal of the Plan, namely, to assist the Hispanic people "in their efforts to achieve integration and participation in the life of our Church and in the building of the Kingdom of God." [#3] The meaning of "integration" is made more precise. Assimilation, the so-called American "melting pot," is categorically rejected, and the bishops continue to say:

---

60. Abp. Sanchez, S.E.P.I. video, Nov. 1987.

By integration we mean that our Hispanic people are to be welcomed to our Church institutions at all levels. They are to be served in their language when possible, and their cultural values and religious traditions are to be respected. Beyond that, we must work toward mutual enrichment through interaction among all our cultures. Our physical facilities are to be made accessible to the Hispanic community. Hispanic participation in the institutions, programs, and activities of the Church is to be constantly encouraged and appreciated. This plan attempts to organize and direct how best to accomplish this integration. [#4]

Turning to the methodology of the Plan, the bishops first traced the Plan's origins to their own pastoral letter of 1983. No mention is made of the processes of the First and Second Encuentros, which had been so important in the coming of age of the Hispanic community. But with regard to the Third Encuentro, they reiterated their aim to take its conclusions seriously and to implement them by means of a "synthesis" of that gathering's prophetic pastoral guidelines. [#5] Although they did not explicitly aver a theology of inculturation, they did claim that the NPPHM "takes into account the sociocultural reality of our Hispanic people and suggests a style of pastoral ministry and model of Church in harmony with their faith and culture." [#5] Moreover, they recognized that this claim "requires an explicit affirmation of the concept of cultural pluralism in our Church within a fundamental unity of doctrine." [#5] This affirmation in turn led the bishops to embrace the method of a "*Pastoral de Conjunto*," i.e., a coordination of all pastoral efforts within the common vision and common objectives set forth in the Plan. The Plan was to be "at the service of the *Pastoral de Conjunto*," and the elements of planning for this collaboration include:

- analysis of reality wherein the Church must carry out her mission;
- reflection on this reality in light of the Gospel and the teachings of the Church;
- commitment to action resulting from this reflection;
- pastoral theological reflection on this process;
- development of a pastoral plan;
- implementation;
- ongoing evaluation of what is being done;
- and, the celebration of the accomplishment of this life experience, always within the context of prayer and its relationship to life. [#6; emphases mine]

The document provided a simple diagram of this process. (See illustration next page.)

The bishops then turned to the "Framework of Hispanic Reality." A rapid review of the history of the Americas highlighted the mingling of peoples, "a true mestizaje." [#7] Unfortunately there was no attempt at differentiation among the various Hispanic groups. The section contains only a brief admission of the

PASTORAL PLANNING PROCESS

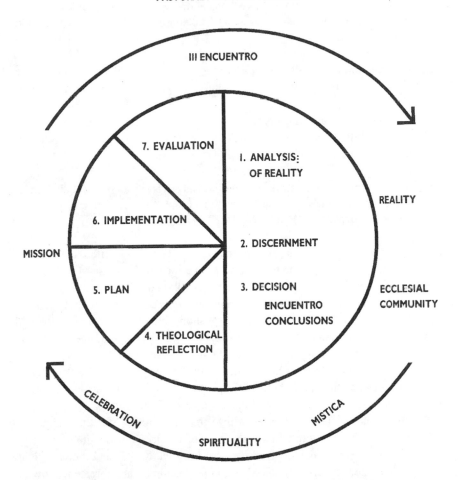

[Figure 3. From *The National Pastoral Plan for Hispanic Ministry*, p. 3.]

Church's failures in service to the indigenous peoples. Likewise, there is only an oblique reference to Anglo cultural oppression of Mexican Americans after Guadalupe Hidalgo. The two Americas were summed up as "a hemisphere of many cultures and three dominant languages," (i.e., Spanish, Portuguese and English), and the bishops concluded:

> Since the Church is the guardian of the mission of Jesus Christ, it must forever accommodate the changing populations and shifting cultures of mankind. To the

extent the Church is impregnated with cultural norms, to that extent it divides and separates; to the extent it replaces cultural norms with the primacy of love, it unites the many into the Body of Christ without dissolving difference or destroying identity. [#9]

Although the tragic mistakes of the past are dealt with gingerly, the bishops clearly wanted to situate themselves today within a heightened consciousness of the plurality of cultures.

Turning to culture, the bishops noted the continuing vitality of Hispanic culture in the United States. They signalled respect for the theological significance of culture when they stated:

Culture primarily expresses how people live and perceive the world, one another, and God. Culture is the set of values by which a people judge, accept, and live what is considered important within the community. [#10]

They then reviewed the cultural values they had previously identified in their 1983 pastoral letter: respect for the person, deep love for family, sense of community, appreciation for the gift of life and authentic devotion to Mary.

The document's look at the Hispanic situation concluded with a glance at other aspects of the social reality. Here the bishops found a young population with many recent immigrants, suffering from poor education and unemployment. Numerous problems beset the Hispanic family. Despite vital popular religious practices and evident interest in spirituality, the bishops noted sadly that 88% of Hispanics are not active in Catholic parishes, with participation sparsest among the poor, among men and in the generations beyond the first.[61]

The bishops then followed with some comments on the "Doctrinal Framework." The section actually opens with remarks on the situation of the Hispanic people within the larger context of U.S. society. "The Catholic heritage and cultural identity of Hispanics," said the bishops, "are threatened by the prevailing secular values of the American society." [#12] Denouncing the poverty and marginalization which have been the lot of Hispanics, the bishops now looked to this people as "a prophetic presence in the face of the materialism and individualism of society" and "a source of renewal within the Catholic Church in North America." [#12]

Ecclesiological foundations were then laid. The Church's mission, in the authors' view, is to continue the work of Jesus, i.e., "to announce the Kingdom of God and the means for entering it." [#13] The Church does so "by entering into the

---

61. NPPHM, #11, p. 5; the document relies on Roberto Gonzalez and Michael LaVelle, *The Hispanic Catholic in the United States: A Socio-Cultural and Religious Profile* (N.Y.: Northeast Catholic Pastoral Center for Hispanics, 1985).

cultural, religious, and social reality of the people, becoming incarnate in and with the people." [#13] In its "prophetic voice" denouncing sin and announcing hope, "the Church continues to make an option for the poor and the marginalized." [#14] In its "identity with the risen Christ" the Church looks to "a new social order" and even "a new style of Church as leaven." [#14] The bishops traced the Church's "solidarity" and the "coresponsibility" shared by all for the mission to the action of the Holy Spirit. [#15]

The doctrinal section was followed by a very brief section on spirituality, or *mística*. The bishops gave this definition of spirituality:

> Spirituality is understood to be the way of life of a people, a movement by the Spirit of God, and the grounding of one's identity as a Christian in every circumstance of life. It is the struggle to live the totality of one's personal and communitarian life in keeping with the Gospel; spirituality is the orientation and perspective of all the dimensions of a person's life in the following of Jesus and in continuous dialogue with the Father. [#16]

They then affirmed, in a general way, the prophetic pastoral guidelines of the Third Encuentro as an authentic expression of and contribution to the spirituality of the Hispanic people at this time in history.

Curiously, the matter of spirituality was taken up again at somewhat greater length in a concluding section of the document. [#93-101] Here the authors identified five prominent aspects of Hispanic spirituality. The first was a vital "sense of the presence of God" that is at once transcendent and imminent. Secondly they noted Hispanics' lively devotion to the Virgin Mary; surprisingly, there was no consideration of the special importance of Our Lady of Guadalupe. In the third place the bishops saw that this spirituality is woven into the fabric of everyday life through the importance ascribed to home, family, relationships and community. Fourthly, one of the sources of this spirituality is identified as the "pre-Hispanic cultures," elements of which have been assumed into Hispanic popular devotions and culture. Finally, the bishops praised the rich panoply of Hispanic popular religious expression. They expressed the belief that these customs both fortify one for life's difficulties and inspire the struggle for justice. The bishops further stated their hope that the NPPHM can serve as a "source of evangelization" for popular religion and an impetus for the enrichment of liturgy with appropriate cultural expressions. They then affirmed what they saw as a growth beyond "personal and family spirituality" into a more "communitarian and ecclesial" and socially-conscious spirituality through the Third Encuentro. And they closed by reiterating that the NPPHM is rooted in the history and reflection of the Hispanic people themselves.

Having laid some concise, foundational remarks on the history, culture, spirituality and social reality of the Hispanic people on the one hand, and on the mission of the Church on the other, the document then set forth its "General Objective." It reads:

> To live and promote by means of a *Pastoral de Conjunto* a model of church that is: communitarian, evangelizing, and missionary; incarnate in the reality of the Hispanic people and open to the diversity of cultures; a promoter and example of justice; active in developing leadership through integral education; leaven for the Kingdom of God in society. [#17]

No explanatory remarks accompany this fecund statement. Its ambitious program is worked out in four areas of more specific objectives and programs.

The first dimension is entitled "*Pastoral de Conjunto*: From Fragmentation to Coordination." The bishops admitted that common vision and coordination are often lacking among laity, clergy and religious. [#19] The objective, they said, is to assist the Hispanic people in living "Church as communion." [#20-1] They called upon the Secretariat for Hispanic Affairs to lead the way in integrating the vision of the NPPHM in the structures of the NCCB/USCC, and upon bishops, diocesan and parish officials to do the same on their levels. [#22-3] They called for more Hispanic leadership to participate in decision-making at all levels and for the promotion of greater understanding and communion among cultural groups. [#24-5] They saw a need for the creation of more diocesan Hispanic pastoral offices and for improved cooperation among these offices. [#26]

The bishops also made a significant call upon each diocese to move toward *pastoral de conjunto* by creating its own diocesan pastoral plan for implementing the NPPHM "according to its own reality." [#27] They even hoped for area or parish pastoral plans for implementing the diocesan plans. [#28] They made a specific plea for "diocesan and area coordination among small ecclesial communities" through meetings of coordinators designed to foster a shared missionary vision. [#29] The bishops asked for more pastoral and theological formation and training programs for Hispanic pastoral agents at all levels. [#30-2] Finally, they called for increased communication among groups, movements and SECs through leadership gatherings, common projects, newsletters and increased use of the mass media. [#33-6]

The second dimension of the Plan was entitled "Evangelization: From a Place to a Home." In a background section, the bishops began by admitting that "the great majority of our Hispanic people feel distant or marginated from the Catholic Church." [#37] While stressing that the parish remains "the basic organizational unit of the Church," the U.S. bishops also affirmed that "conversion and a sense of being Church are often best lived out in smaller communities within the parish which are more personal and offer a greater sense of belonging." [#37] The bishops took note of the Third Encuentro's efforts to promote small communities, and of the efforts of "many apostolic movements and church organizations" which have provided spiritual enrichment in small group settings over the years, and they affirmed all of these as effective tools of evangelization. [#38] Then, for the second of four times in the document, they took note of the urgent need for efforts to respond to the proselytism of various sects and fundamentalist groups.[62]

The background was followed by a "specific objective":

> To recognize, develop, accompany, and support small ecclesial communities and other Church groups (e.g., *Cursillos de Cristiandad, Movimiento Familiar Cristiano*, RENEW, Charismatic Movement, prayer groups, etc.), which in union with the bishop are effective instruments of evangelization for the Hispanic people. These small ecclesial communities and other groups within the parish framework promote experiences of faith and conversion, prayer life, missionary outreach and evangelization, interpersonal relations and fraternal love, prophetic questioning and actions for justice. They are a prophetic challenge for the renewal of our Church and humanization of our society. [#40]

This objective is the centerpiece of the entire section on evangelization; indeed its influence over the other three sections can be detected as well. Two concerns on the part of the bishops are immediately evident here. One is to be as inclusive as possible, respecting the various movements and spiritualities and styles of small communities that exist within the Hispanic community. A second is to keep all these groups in some way related to the institutional structure, particularly the parish. Given these understandable concerns, the very positive embrace of the SECs and other groups as a "prophetic challenge" to both Church and society is even more remarkable.

To achieve this objective of fostering evangelization through SECs and other groups, the Plan envisioned several programs and projects. It called for a "think tank" of pastoral agents with SEC experience to write a workbook of guidelines and practical aids for development of SECs.[63] This was to be followed by a "national training session" for leaders from all regions, the purpose of which would be "to develop a common vision and methodology in the formation and support of small ecclesial communities." [#42] Dioceses were also urged to sponsor theological reflections on evangelization and SECs. [#43]

On the local level, the bishops called for parishes to be "missionary" in character primarily through promotion of SECs. [#44] This amounted to re-

---

62. NPPHM #39; also nos. 5, 44, 83.

63. NPPHM #41, p. 12. Such a symposium was in fact held in 1989 under the auspices of the Secretariat for Hispanic Affairs. A scaled-down version of the workbook was published later: *Communion and Mission* (Washington: USCC, 1996).

envisioning the parish as a "community of communities." [#47] Such parishes would exude "a welcoming and inclusive atmosphere that is culturally sensitive to the marginated." [#45] They would offer ongoing formation for evangelization to existing groups, and place a high priority on organizing visitation to homes of the marginalized, drawing them into SECs. [#46, 48-9] This new umbrella model of parish was also to cultivate the connections between faith and social justice as an integral component of its evangelizing thrust in all parish programs, but especially through SECs. [#50]

The missionary and social-justice orientation of the Church received further attention in the third area of the Plan, "Missionary Option: From Pews to Shoes." Here the bishops took up and affirmed the missionary priorities embraced at the Third Encuentro: the poor and marginalized, the family, women and youth. After reviewing the obstacles faced by each of these groups [#51-5], they endorsed this "specific objective":

> To promote faith and effective participation in church and societal structures on the part of these priority groups (the poor, women, families, youth) so that they may be agents of their own destiny (self-determination) and capable of progressing and becoming organized. [#56]

Ten specific steps were endorsed for the purpose of achieving this broad objective of participation and self-determination. The USCC Office of the Pastoral Care of Migrants and Refugees was to have one full-time person coordinate and evaluate ministry to migrant farmworkers through semi-annual meetings with representatives of all regions. [#57] More vaguely, the bishops promised to step up social justice and community organizing efforts at all levels. [#58] They called for greater attention to the large number of Hispanics found in the armed services. [#59] With regard to families, the bishops promised to organize a national forum which would analyze family needs, assist in setting pastoral goals and issue materials usable in SECs and other local groups. [#60-2]

On the subject of women, the NPPHM envisioned a series of regional meetings for those engaged in ministry to women. Four goals were given for these gatherings. They were to:

> • Analyze the situation of Hispanic women to manifest more clearly their gifts of intelligence and compassion, which they share with the Church;
> • Identify a model of Church that nourishes and fosters ministries by women;
> • Value the role of the small ecclesial community in the promotion of women;
> • Examine, in light of the process of the III Encuentro, the reality of the Hispanic woman and consider which ministries should be maintained and which should be created. [#63]

Nothing further was specified about the number of such meetings, nor about how they were to go about achieving this ambitious agenda.

Three steps were addressed to the area of Hispanic youth ministry. The first was a nebulous encouragement of "organisms of coordination" at all levels to cultivate greater participation of Hispanic youth in the Church. [#64] The second asked for more networking among youth ministers in order to share successful strategies (SECs mentioned among them) by which youth can be welcomed and offered formation and opportunities for service. [#65] The last called for the convocation of a national youth encuentro to take up broad issues related to the direction of ministry among Hispanic youth. [#66]

The final area addressed by the NPPHM was "Formation: From Good Will to Skills." The bishops saw a critical lack of both pastoral ministers – so critical that it made "uncertain the survival of the Catholic faith among Hispanics" [#67] – and of programs of spirituality and catechesis. [#68] Their "specific objective" was:

> To provide leadership formation adapted to the Hispanic culture in the United States that will help people to live and promote a style of Church which will be a leaven of the Kingdom of God in society. [#69]

Fifteen projects and programs were proposed. The bishops wanted to foster heightened "conscientization" through increased "theological-pastoral reflection" at the local and regional levels. [#70-1] They also called for more scientific study of the "socioeconomic, cultural, religious, and psychological aspects" of Hispanic life, especially the family, youth, women, popular religion and the poor. [#72] To achieve this goal they promised to seek graduate research scholarships.

Four steps were endorsed for the fostering of Hispanic vocations to the clergy and religious life. The bishops promised culturally-sensitive vocation promotion, especially through involving Hispanic lay men and women in the recruitment process. [#73] They sought to get the topic of vocations on the agenda of Hispanic lay organizations. [#74] They recognized a special need for more training of diocesan and religious vocation directors for work among Hispanics. [#75] In addition, they asked for wider implementation of an existing parish-based program by which parishioners are asked to identify possible vocation candidates. [#76]

Five of the steps sought to address the needs for leadership formation among Hispanics. The first of these specifically addressed the need for leaders to "create, encourage, and coordinate small ecclesial communities." [#77] A second step sought development of a program of education on the dignity of women, to be implemented among the SECs. [#78] A task force was to be named to design a formation program for adult youth ministers and youth leaders. [#79] The bishops asked seminaries, religious communities and formation programs for the permanent diaconate to incorporate the conclusions and vision of the III Encuentro. [#80]

They also pled for more education of both Hispanic and non-Hispanic pastoral ministers in the history, culture, needs and "pastoral principles" of Hispanics. [#81]

Finally the bishops addressed the relative dearth of materials and programs for various needs among Hispanics. They asked publishers and pastoral institutes for more popular materials written for Hispanics in the SECs in a variety of areas: Bible study, social analysis, SECs, immigration, political rights and participation, parenting and family planning, popular religion and liturgy. [#82, 84] They promised a national meeting of pastoral ministers to reflect on and prepare a response to non-Catholic proselytism among Hispanics. [#83] This national gathering was to issue materials and prepare mobile teams to address this issue with pastoral agents on the local level.

In all four areas, after each specific project or program the "responsible agents" for that item were listed. These range from local pastoral agents and collaborators to parishes, dioceses, regional pastoral institutes, several organs of the USCC and the bishops themselves, and various combinations thereof. The question of the timing for fulfilment of the commitment is addressed in each case in the same way: "*When*: In accordance with the normal channels for plans and programs and budget procedures of the respective entities involved." In his presentation of the Plan to the NCCB at the November 1987 meeting, Archbishop Sanchez had addressed the concern raised by some of his peers about funding for the Plan's implementation in a time of financial constraint. He explained that the drafting committee had decided against seeking special funding, preferring instead to work through existing channels, at least for the time being.[64] Clearly Sanchez' remarks were designed to allay fears about approving the Plan on account of its possible financial implications. The possibility of revisiting the national funding question at a later time was, however, left open.

A concluding section of the document addressed the issue of evaluation. It began, "Evaluation is an integral part of pastoral planning," and envisioned the future possibility of "reshaping the Plan in the light of ongoing pastoral experiences." [#85] It cautioned that such evaluation must take place within the same kind of constructive atmosphere or *mística* that marked the Third Encuentro. [#86] The "specific objective" of such evaluation was:

> To determine if the general objective of the plan is being attained and whether the process faithfully reflects what the Church is and does in relation to the Kingdom. [#87]

Five steps follow. A "National Advisory Committee" was to be appointed to facilitate the evaluation effort and compile its results. [#88] Educational workshops

---

64. Abp. Sanchez, S.E.P.I. video, Nov. 1987.

on the value and method of the evaluation process were to be held for diocesan personnel. [#89] Then evaluation meetings at the diocesan, regional and finally national levels were to be held. [#90-2] The diocesan meetings were to be comprised of parish and SEC representatives, and the regional meetings of diocesan representatives. The national meeting was to gather representatives of all regions and issue a written evaluation report.

CHAPTER FOUR

Evaluating the Plan as an Instance of Local Theology

Can the *National Pastoral Plan for Hispanic Ministry* lead to an authentically inculturated pastoral praxis in the Mexican American cultural milieu? That is the question to be explored in this chapter.

It has to be admitted at the outset that neither a definitive nor a completely comprehensive answer can be rendered to the question. This is so in part because inculturation by its own nature remains an open and ongoing process. In addition, an evaluation of the NPPHM could not be definitive without an enormous amount of field research. One would have to study in considerable breadth and detail the pastoral praxis which is actually being engendered by the Plan in local Mexican American communities across the country in order to reach a verdict. And, even if one were to garner such huge amounts of field data, the complex nature of pastoral practice and the multitude of local circumstances which impinge upon it would preclude any illusions about a truly comprehensive judgment. So the ambition of this chapter is more modest. I hope to give some necessarily provisional, critical reflections on the NPPHM in relation to the Mexican American community and its aspirations for an inculturated Catholic Christian faith.

This chapter's goal will be approached through Schreiter's "map" for inculturated local theology. We trace the NPPHM and its formulation through the steps outlined by Schreiter and evaluate the Plan in terms of the demands of each step. In somewhat more depth we examine the leading specific strategy endorsed by the Plan, the formation of small ecclesial communities (SECs), and offer some reflections on that particular strategy in relation to the issues of inculturation among Mexican Americans. After we have stepped through Schreiter's map, our findings may be summarized by a brief return to the evaluative criteria Schreiter suggested, inquiring into the adequacy of the NPPHM with regard to those criteria.

The Starting Point

Schreiter points out that local theological reflection and pastoral praxis do not begin "*de novo*" in a vacuum. [26] Communities reach toward new theological understandings which help them make better sense out of local circumstances or challenges. Often, says the author, the process of local theology is set in motion by one of three things. First, a community may grow in self-awareness of their cultural and/or their religious identity and so begin to call into question the existing theologies they have received. Schreiter cites the example of an African religious leader who wishes to develop a more inculturated liturgical style, but who must confront an established popular predilection for Latin hymnody.

A second triggering factor could be an event or development in the culture, such as a political or economic crisis, a labor strike, or the reality of some form of oppression by a foreign power or an elite or both. A third possibility is that a local community confronts theological developments taking place in other local churches, or on a wider ecclesial scale, and a response is prompted. The directives of the Second Vatican Council would be one obvious example of this. Thus, as Schreiter says, "beginning points can arise from previous theologies, from the culture, or from church tradition." [26]

In the case of the Hispanic community in the United States, including the Mexican Americans, I believe that one can observe all three of these starting points. In the first place, there is more than ample evidence that Latinos, and especially Mexican Americans, have been becoming increasingly conscious of themselves as a people through most of this century. This growth in awareness has patently resulted in increasing dissatisfaction with being second-class members of their own Church. Mexican Americans perceive a serious disjunction between the theologies embedded within their own popular religiosity and cultural values, and the theology which governs the structures of the U.S. Catholic Church down to and including the parish level. The reigning theology has more and more been felt to be inadequate, foreign, Anglo and ignorant of Hispanic needs and aspirations. Unfortunately, this heightened awareness finds only a muted voice in the Plan itself, which does little to admit the cultural failures of the Church in the past. However, there is no doubt that the cry of dissatisfaction with the received theology made itself known vociferously through all three of the national Encuentro processes.

Secondly, I believe there are three interrelated cultural crises which Mexican Americans have confronted which have spawned new theological thinking. One is the growing awareness that they have been and still are a marginated people within the wider scope of U.S. society. They have learned their own oppressive history, and the tools of the social sciences have revealed with abundant clarity that they lag behind the majority in nearly every category. On this point the Plan is somewhat stronger, retelling the historical narrative in more accurate fashion. It firmly endorses ongoing efforts on behalf of social liberation. At some basic levels the Plan is clearly not ignorant of the fruits of social scientific research.

A second cultural crisis derives from the assimilative constraints of the dominant culture. Hispanics, Mexican Americans among them, continue to experience considerable pressure to conform to Anglo culture in a myriad of ways, in the media, on the job, in the marketplace and even in their religious beliefs and practices. Undeniably assimilation has been occurring, especially among the younger generations who have lived their whole lives in the U.S. The Spanish language is lost, Mexican family cohesion and customs are weakened, and religious patterns change. In the NPPHM the U.S. bishops issue a strong, if belated, protest against this cultural tyranny.

A third cultural crisis is being provoked by the inroads made among Hispanics by fundamentalist, pentecostal and sectarian religious groups. Mexican American Catholic leaders view the success of these groups in winning converts with considerable alarm. The concern is due in part to the fact that the religious migration exposes the inadequacy of Catholic pastoral praxis. As Allan Deck continues to remind us, Mexican Americans are finding something in the storefront churches that they are not finding in Catholic parishes.[1] But the alarm also stems from the fact that Catholicism and Mexican culture have a longstanding marriage and so have been viewed as inseparable from one another. Rightly or wrongly, a threat to ethnic religious identity is thus also assumed to be a threat to cultural identity. In the NPPHM this alarm becomes a reechoed theme for the bishops too.

As to Schreiter's third starting point, one can readily observe the transparent influence of theological developments taking place in the wider Catholic Church upon both the Encuentro process and the resulting planning document. Vatican II – especially the affirmation of cultural pluralism in *Gaudium et Spes* and *Ad Gentes,* and *Gaudium et Spes*'s calls for engagement with the problems and hopes of the world and for a more participative and collaborative style of ministry – spawned an enormous amount of fresh and creative theological and pastoral reflection in wide sectors of the Church. The Council's impact can be traced in the actions of the U.S. bishops themselves in devoting greater attention to Hispanic concerns. Similarly, it is reflected in the spontaneous efforts of groups like PADRES and Las Hermanas and in the First Encuentro itself. The very notion of an inculturated pastoral plan would surely not have been possible in the Church were it not for the ways in which, as we have seen, the Council called for serious and respectful study of and dialogue with culture. The Third Encuentro's repeated call for a *pastoral de conjunto*, endorsed in the Plan, reflects the marked influence of the "People of God" ecclesiology of both *Lumen Gentium* and *Gaudium et Spes*.

In addition, developments taking place in Latin America have been well known in the U.S. Hispanic community, as we have also seen. In the conclusions of the Third Encuentro and in the NPPHM as well one finds the language of liberation and the preferential option for the poor, themes sounded insistently by Latin American theologians over the past thirty years. These same themes have resonated on an official level at all of the CELAM conferences from Medellín to Santo Domingo. Liberation theology, Medellín and Puebla have all been powerful

---

1. See, e.g., Deck, "Proselytism and Hispanic Catholics: How Long Can We Cry Wolf?" *America* 159 (10 Dec. 1988) 485-90.

forces on the U.S. Hispanic scene, and one does not have to look far in the NPPHM to trace their influence.

All of the factors mentioned so far interlock with one another. One can see this most vividly in even a cursory examination of the documents produced by all three Encuentros. While one or the other of them may have predominated at one time or event or stage in the process, or in the motivation of particular participants, all of them converge in spurring a process of doing theology in an inculturated or contextualized way. That process resulted in, among other things, the NPPHM. Admittedly the capstone document does not reflect each of these motivating factors or starting points equally well. But there can be little doubt that the Plan is indebted to all of them.

Step #1: Previous Local Theologies

The first movement of Schreiter's map is to take note of previous local theologies. This means taking stock of the theologies already operative in the environment. As we have seen, the Hispanic community, including the Mexican Americans, found themselves confronted with an entrenched, authoritative theology in the Anglo church, a theology which, for the reasons listed above, was found to be inadequate. We have also noted the existence of previous theology encoded within the popular religiosity and culture of the Mexican American community itself and the discontinuity and conflict experienced between this theology and the one officially in place. Nor is the theology held by Mexican Americans themselves immune to criticism. In the writings of Allan Deck, for example, and to a lesser extent Virgilio Elizondo, one detects some ambivalence toward what prevails among their own people. There is strong attachment to and defense of that heritage's positive values and the way it makes Mexican American identity distinct. At the same time there is admission that Mexican Americans have too often been passive, even complicit, in the face of their own oppression. This can perhaps be traced both to a degree of tacit acceptance of the dominant culture's theology and to the irenic aspect of the Mexican temperament itself. One sees the ambivalence clearly, for example, in the treatment of popular religion by Deck, Elizondo, Rodriguez and other Mexican American writers. Some equivocation is to be expected, of course, not least because we find it mirrored in the larger discourse of Latin American liberation theology.

Step #2: Cultural Analysis

Schreiter's second step asks us to consider the opening of culture. A few points have already been made. As we saw, consciousness of cultural identity has been growing steadily among all Hispanics in this century, especially since the civil rights struggles of the 1960s. The fact of cultural pluralism and the need for a more penetrating grasp of culture have come into vogue in many quarters, including the Church. Much has been written and said about Mexican American culture in recent years, and an enormous fund of cultural insight fed into the efforts of the three Encuentros. The structure of the Second and Third Encuentros, especially the wide net of participation they cast, ensured to some extent that common Hispanic values were identified and honored, as were common experiences of margination. Statistical population studies and other forms of sociological data have been widely disseminated, and they are evident in both the Encuentro documents and the final Plan. The Encuentros and the formulation of the Plan form a single, continuous narrative. This narrative is an enormously powerful experience of cultural analysis and affirmation, as many participants in these events attest.

But, despite these very significant advances, and with the assistance of hindsight, there remain reasons to judge that the cultural analysis behind the NPPHM is still somewhat superficial and imbalanced. One can see this, for example, in the brevity of the document's "Framework of Hispanic Reality" section. Of course, this section is intended to be merely suggestive, a quick summary of a much larger body of cultural reflection having taken place through the Encuentro process. But the historical background given is so rapid that it appears almost facile. Moreover, its treatment of the Church's role in that history is extremely selective. It highlights the positive accomplishments while overlooking both the Church's complicity in colonialism and the Church's own tarnished record of discrimination and neglect. It is difficult to see how this legacy can be overcome without a greater degree of official candor.

The sections on culture and the social reality are even less adequate. Although some important Hispanic values are noted, as are some of the salient features of the Hispanic social situation, they are listed tersely and only rarely appear elsewhere in the document. Once again, it is undoubtedly true that cultural and social assessment do inform the document, at least indirectly, through the Encuentro process. But the debt is not sufficiently acknowledged. One cannot help but notice the striking contrast on this score between the NPPHM and the document of the Third Encuentro. The latter document alludes to the relevant cultural and social data repeatedly. In fact, the Third Encuentro was methodical in doing so: each major area of the "Commitments" section opens with a subsection labeled "Looking at Our Reality" or the like.[2]

From the vantage point of the theology of inculturation, "thick description" of the cultural systems is methodologically indispensable. At no stage of the process culminating in the NPPHM does there appear to have been a truly thorough, systematic attempt at social or cultural analysis. The result is that even in the document of the Third Encuentro the social and cultural segments retain a

---

2. *Prophetic Voices*, pp. 7, 9, 10, 11, 13-4.

fragmentary and anecdotal quality. The NPPHM is hobbled by a more serious liability of this omission: the descriptions of the cultural and social reality, together with the description of Hispanic spirituality or *mística*, can appear as mere ornamentation, marginal to the overall project. Thus, the process should have included a more thoroughgoing, scientific study of both the cultural identity and social reality of Hispanics. In short, the NPPHM does not benefit from all the help it should get from the social sciences. Moreover, it does not even respect, in an explicit and deliberate way, the sources that it does in fact utilize and depend upon, e.g., the participants in the consultations leading up to the Third Encuentro. It might also have mentioned gratefully the pioneering work of Elizondo, Deck and other prominent Hispanic writers who have described the Hispanic reality and brought it to the Church's attention.

Part of the difficulty inheres in the generic, one-size-fits-all character of the very term *Hispanic*. *Hispanic* (the same can be said for *Latino/a*) is an adjective applied to anyone whose ethnic origin can be traced to a Latin American country. Thus, it includes a very broad ethnic panoply: Mexicans, Puerto Ricans, Cubans, Dominicans, Spaniards, Guatemalans, Nicaraguans, Panamanians, Colombians, etc. As one historian writes, "It is a mistake to lump all Latin Americans together, since they have separate histories that must be respected."[3]   Furthermore, among the Mexican cohort one finds still more diversity. They run the gamut from recently arrived immigrants, both legal and illegal, many of whom speak only Spanish, through second-generation folk and beyond. Indeed some of them are people whose families have lived in what is now the Southwest United States for nearly four centuries and who speak only English.

What justification can there be for bundling all these people together? On a number of informal occasions I have posed this very question to Hispanic leaders themselves. Consistently they respond first by defending the term *Hispanic* and its employment, and the parameters it defines, in the pastoral planning process and elsewhere. They cite powerful commonalities of language, religion, values and customs. They speak of common experiences of immigration, discrimination, poverty and minority status. Defense of the univocal meaning of *Hispanic* seems to be even more vigorous among those who have participated in the consensus- and coalition-building experiences of the regional and national Encuentros.

But, when pressed, these same sources will often admit that the pluralism embraced by the term *Hispanic* has been and often still is problematic. The history of the Encuentros and of the Plan itself is, in part, a complex story of compromise among ethnic groups whose interests and needs, while convergent in the main, diverge in some nonetheless important ways. Only once does the Plan itself acknowledge this, when it identifies a need "to forge unity among all Hispanics who

---

3. Acuña, p. x.

have come from the entire spectrum of the Spanish-speaking world." [#12] Significant differences of values, style and custom do exist among these groups. Mexican Americans and Cuban Americans, for example, whatever they may have in common, are quite different culturally, economically and socially – even a superficial acquaintance of these two peoples learns that early on. Understandably, some of the differences had to be ignored or papered over in order to achieve the vital objectives embodied by the national pastoral plan. However, one has to question whether some factors of critical value to the project of a fully inculturated theology and pastoral praxis may have been lost along the way.

Cultural analysis is a many-faceted task. In Chapter 2 we identified some of the religious patterns, cultural values and socioeconomic realities which shape Mexican American life. We may now inquire as to whether these factors are adequately encompassed by the NPPHM.

Religion

Turning first to the religious dimension, perhaps the most poignant question to ask is this: does the Plan redress the neglect and discrimination which we have identified as main characteristics of the Mexican American experience within the U.S. Catholic Church? To a great extent the answer to this question can be in the affirmative. Taken as a whole, as we have seen, the Encuentro process gradually migrated from a spontaneous movement at the margins into the Church's official embrace. The resulting Plan, although not perfectly consonant with the conclusions of the final Encuentro, does demonstrate that those conclusions were taken with a high degree of seriousness by the bishops. Both the encouragement of the process and the promulgation of a document which promises so many new pastoral initiatives do bespeak a strong commitment at high levels to attend to Hispanic needs and to incorporate Hispanic Catholics more closely into the Church.

If all of the strategies of the NPPHM are implemented, or even most of them, the Catholic Church in the United States may yet become a much more solicitous faith home for Hispanic Catholics, including Mexican Americans. They will be served more often in their language, catechized in ways more attuned to their culture, and invited to greater participation and leadership within a more collaborative style of ministry. Inculturated evangelization of Mexican Americans will be a high priority, and Mexican Americans will find in their Church a powerful ally in their struggle for social equality. Mexican American youth, women, migrant workers and immigrants can all expect to receive greater respect and attention from the Church because of the Plan.

There is no doubt that the NPPHM represents a huge stride forward for Hispanics generally and for Mexican Americans in particular. This is seen most clearly when one considers the Plan as almost a *creatio ex nihilo*, in two ways. For one, whereas certain improvised or provisional local methods for addressing ethnic needs had been the rule for previous waves of immigrants to the U.S. (e.g., national parishes, sodalities, etc.), Hispanics have largely been deprived even of those. Their experience has consistently been one of being ignored on all levels, so that the Plan represents a radically new attitude on the part of the Church. Secondly, it is clear that nothing like the Plan has been attempted before; the very genre is new. The NPPHM is a first venture into concerted pastoral planning respecting the parameters and contours of a given cultural milieu. As such, the Plan has to be acknowledged and applauded as a break with past practice, an initial step into a quite different *modus operandi*. The hope expressed by the present author for greater methodological sophistication and thoroughness in future such planning efforts in no way diminishes the affirmation that the NPPHM represents a promising departure into new territory.

However, with regard to the Mexican American context, a host of questions remains. One doubts, for example, whether the Plan does enough to reform parish structures to meet the needs of Mexican Americans. The Plan does make a clear call for the parish to become more welcoming, more evangelizing and more pluralistic as a "community of communities." But does this go far enough, especially for a population whose traditional ties to the parish structure are not strong? However well intentioned, is it not still tantamount to inviting Hispanics to blend into the Anglo church, rather than letting Hispanics have and be their own church? How can Mexican American identity be respected and preserved in this setting? Recall Deck's complaint about the omission of national parishes for Hispanics. Why was this strategy, so successful in aiding earlier ethnic communities in the U.S., passed over both in the Plan and in the Third Encuentro?

One strongly suspects that at least one piece of the answer to that question is the clergy shortage, especially the severe shortage of Spanish-speaking priests. The bishops simply do not have the personnel to staff new parishes – at least not in the traditional manner, which insists, among other things, upon celibate men only. Even laying aside the question of qualifications for priestly ministry and the question of erecting national parishes, one may ask whether the Plan goes far enough in addressing the urgent need for more Hispanic vocations. Hispanics voiced a strong desire to be served by their own. Indigenous ministry performs a profoundly important symbolic function in every cultural community.[4] The NPPHM acknowledges the need for more Hispanic clergy, but makes only rather vague appeals for greater recruitment efforts. It offers little help in identifying or overcoming existing obstacles to such efforts, nor incentive for more men to accept that call.

---

4. See Carl F. Starkloff, "Keepers of Tradition: The Symbol Power of Indigenous Ministry," *Kérygma* 23:52 (1989) 3-120.

Earlier we identified a number of religious customs and movements integral to the faith of Mexican Americans. The relationship of this popular religiosity to the aims of the Plan is not at all clear. In fact, the whole treatment of spirituality in the Plan is puzzling. Two sections on this subject, as we saw, are used to bracket the whole, but in between there is little that draws water from this well. There are also some noteworthy lacunae. Where, for instance, is Guadalupe? In the entire document I can find only one invocation of the Mother of Jesus under the title most dear to Mexican Americans [#2], and only two other very brief mentions of the importance of Mary for these Christians. [#10, 94] A possible explanation for this glaring omission lies in the fact that, again, the Plan is aimed at all Hispanics rather than at Mexican Americans only. Perhaps this is one of the places where the peculiarities of the Mexican American element were lost in the process of melding their voice with the voices of other groups for whom Guadalupe is not so central to their identity and faith. But we must still ask, how can one hope to construct an inculturated theology or praxis for mestizo Mexican Americans without speaking about the Brown Virgin of Tepeyac?

One is similarly disappointed with regard to other aspects of popular piety. The Plan offers few insights into its relationship to *Las Posadas, quinceañeras,* devotions to the saints, home altars, etc. Its conspicuous intent to bolster family life offers some implicit support, but that is all. The same goes for the movements (*Cursillo*, charismatic renewal, etc.) which play such a large role in the faith lives of so many Mexican Americans. There is neither affirmation of the positive values of these practices, nor any attempt to address the need we recognized earlier for some appropriate guidance or correction to their excesses. There is simply no direct attempt to integrate the goals and strategies of the Plan with these aspects of popular religion.

In an earlier section we summarily characterized Mexican American religiosity as vivid, affective, spontaneous, communal, participative and sacramental. In many respects the Plan seems an ill-suited kind of instrument for this target group. The document has an institutional, even bureaucratic, flavor that is in marked contrast to the spontaneous, affective and non-institutional character of Mexican American culture and religiosity. As one observer put it, to some extent "the means are at odds with the ends" in the Plan.

The bishops and many Mexican American leaders both have pinned their hopes on the cultivation of small communities to provide a context within which a culturally authentic style of spirituality may be expressed and developed. As small, informal, flexible spaces, SECs certainly nurture many of the things dear to Mexican Americans: personal contact, affectivity, communality and participation. SECs represent one means of cultivating relationships and a sense of belonging, giving the Church the welcoming, intimate, personal face for which so many Mexican Americans long.

On the other hand, however, SECs also represent a spiritual path that in some respects would seem to run counter to the cultural predispositions of Mexican Americans. SECs are more Word-centered than is common within any of the Latino groups. They utilize discussion as a means of connecting biblical texts with everyday life. The style of Hispanic piety generally, including that of Mexican Americans, is neither discursive nor heavily reliant on scriptural texts. It may be that SECs will be most successful among Mexican Americans when they find ways to integrate reverence for the centrality of the Word with the various devotionals and sacramentals which are the ordinary staples of Mexican American piety. If SECs can meet this challenge, their counter-cultural aspect might even provide some helpful corrective and complementarity to the usual temper of Mexican American spirituality.

We also identified one of the larger challenges facing the Church with regard to Mexican Americans as the huge chasm that continues to exist between the whole realm of the "popular" and the "official." It seems reasonable to hope that SECs may also provide a context within which the popular and the official may interact and be reconciled. But neither this hope nor the grounds for it are spelled out clearly in the Plan. And there may well be other, better strategies by which the gap may be closed. The Plan does, for example, have a lot to say about evangelization and catechesis. We might have expected the issue of bridging the popular and the official to be addressed under those headings, but it is absent.

Values

We identified some of the characteristic cultural values of Mexican Americans as these: love of family, hospitality, honor, *machismo*, a sense of the tragic, personalism, a sense of the limitations of time and celebration. Most of these values were quite clearly, even eloquently, articulated in the final document of the Third Encuentro. Presumably they also informed the bishops directly through the Third Encuentro.

But there is disappointingly little to point to in the Plan itself that would indicate to us how seriously those values were taken or the precise manner in which they were incorporated. One is surprised, for example, to find no mention whatsoever of *fiesta*. Nor do we encounter any thought on the difficult pastoral challenges presented by the prevalence of passivity and fatalism (the underside of the tragic).

Indeed I can find only three of these factors explicitly mentioned in the document. Family life is recognized as a value, and the Plan addresses the needs of families a few times. [#10, 53, 60-2] *Machismo* receives only one mention, an entirely negative reference in connection with the problems faced by women. [#54] Nowhere does the Plan specifically address the needs of men, nor the relative absence of Hispanic males in the pews of the Church. The only Hispanic value which receives somewhat sustained recognition in the NPPHM is the centrality of the person and personal relationships. [#10] Most significantly, this personalism is cited both as the cause for a pervasive feeling of alienation from Church structures and as the reason why small communities are urgently needed. [#37-8, 44-50]

On balance, however, taking the document alone as it stands, even the references to these three cultural value structures are somewhat dilute and superficial. The NPPHM could have benefited greatly from a more sustained and systematic reflection on the full range of values which characterize the Hispanic peoples.

Socioeconomic Location

The document is somewhat more astute in taking into account the socioeconomic realities faced by Mexican Americans. We noted, for example, that as a group Mexican Americans face serious economic disadvantages in U.S. society. Recognition of poverty and its relationship to a history of social discrimination are evident at several points in the document.[5] The urgent needs of families, women and migrant workers receive special attention. Pastoral ministers and all the faithful are called to greater conscientization and commitment to work for social justice.

Closely related to poverty in our Mexican American profile was the reality of educational disadvantage. This factor too was recognized by the bishops. Indeed it is probably not too much to say that the single strongest aspect of the NPPHM is its insistent call for the Church to undertake dramatically increased educational initiatives among all Hispanics. Educational, training and formation efforts are promised in at least 39 of the document's 101 sections.[6] These paragraphs seek improvement in a striking variety of areas, from ordained ministry to lay leadership skills to formation for SECs to social analysis to pastoral and theological reflection. The NPPHM envisions a very ambitious educational program.

Earlier we observed the fact that the Mexican American population as a group is quite young. We also noted that the needs of youth and families received considerable attention by the Third Encuentro. The Plan embodies much of that assembly's concern, for it addresses the needs of families and youth in twelve separate sections.[7] (By way of contrast, there is no mention anywhere in the document of the needs of the Hispanic elderly.) The problems of families and youth

---

5. NPPHM #7-8, 49-54, 56-63, 70-2.
6. NPPHM #23, 30-32, 35, 40-48, 50, 59-63, 67-84, 89.
7. NPPHM #10-11, 53, 55, 60-62, 64-66, 79, 84.

are, on balance, sized up accurately and with an appropriate urgency. Most of the programs proposed in response to these needs have to do with education and networking. Of course, the big innovation with regard to youth was the proposed national youth Encuentro. [#66] All of these, but especially the last, could represent significant new pastoral departures for the Church if implemented.

Still, the Plan does seem to have truncated the emphasis given to youth at the Third Encuentro. The Encuentro had adopted a "preferential option for Hispanic youth"[8] as one of its overall "prophetic pastoral guidelines." It followed this by devoting one entire segment of its work to this area, proposing nine separate "commitments" to Hispanic youth. These included a national office, work to change educational systems and leadership formation.[9] In the NPPHM, on the other hand, we find this topic mainly in three fairly brief subsections of the major "Missionary Option" heading. [#64-6] Two of those subsections merely encourage greater youth participation in the Church and greater networking among those engaged in youth ministry, while the third calls for a national youth Encuentro, something the Third Encuentro had not even asked for. The Third Encuentro's demand for greater investment in youth leadership formation was included within a later subsection of the NPPHM which called in a more general way for "elaboration of a program of youth pastoral ministry." [#79] Most of the Encuentro's youth goals were simply mislaid in the transition to the Plan.

In the profile of the Mexican American people given earlier we also noted that a sizeable segment of that community is composed of various types of migrant workers and immigrants. The organizers of the Third Encuentro had taken pains to ensure that these groups were represented at that assembly, and their voices are reflected numerous times in its final document. The NPPHM, however, evinces only scant sensitivity to the needs of these special groups. In an early section, the "continuous flow of immigrants" is recognized as one of the factors of Hispanic social reality. [#11] The Plan calls for increased attention at the national level to the needs of migrant farmworkers through additional staff in the Office of the Pastoral Care of Migrants and Refugees. [#57] It also targets migrants as one of the groups requiring further scientific research. [#72]

But attention to migrants and immigrants is noticeably missing elsewhere in the Plan. Again, most of the Third Encuentro's concerns seem to have been excluded. In addition, we must conclude that neither the NPPHM nor even the Third Encuentro demonstrates a very nuanced understanding of the situation of migrants and immigrants. In neither source do we discern an awareness of the differing types of migrants and immigrants,[10] nor the patterns peculiar to the Mexican cohort. Since the needs of these people differ significantly according to

---

8. *Prophetic Voices* #3.
9. *Prophetic Voices*, pp. 11-3.
10. Deck, *The Second Wave*, pp. 12-9.

ethnicity, family condition, length of stay, etc., the Plan seems unprepared to grasp and deal with the full spectrum of existing pastoral situations.

Three other social factors characterizing Mexican Americans were identified in our earlier profile: mobility, urbanization and geographic concentration. Surprisingly, I can find no mention at all of these factors in the document of the Third Encuentro. A few brief references to the first two appear in the NPPHM [#11, 53], but there is no concerted effort to integrate them into the Plan's conclusions. These are among the NPPHM's most glaring omissions. Mobility and urbanization are two of the salient features of this population, and they distinguish Mexican Americans markedly from the populace of Mexico itself. Mexican immigrants to the U.S. often come from smaller towns and rural areas of Mexico. Even if they come from larger Mexican cities, they are unprepared for the extremely fluid condition of the North American cities in which they make their new homes. The new arrivals are far from their geographic origins and, usually, from their extended (and sometimes also their immediate) families. The high mobility of U.S. society only exacerbates their experience of rootlessness, lack of belonging and instability. The constant movement of people and the urban distances to be overcome both present formidable challenges for local evangelization efforts, such as the organization of ongoing small Christian communities. How did the U.S. bishops envision implementing the ambitious goals of the NPPHM within a mobile, urban environment? We do not know. The NPPHM tells us more about what the Church hopes to do to preserve the cultural heritage of Hispanics than it does about how the Church will assist its Hispanic flock in confronting the challenges of the larger U.S. culture.

Nor is it clear how the Plan may be adapted for the differing geographic locales of this population. The vast majority of Mexican Americans, as we saw, live in just a handful of states. In many areas of the Southwest they represent a large minority of the total population, or even the majority. But small, widely scattered Mexican American communities can be found in nearly every part of the country. The socioeconomic and cultural challenges which confront such communities as a tiny minority in a small city in the Midwest might be in many ways the same as the challenges faced by a well-established community in New Mexico, for example, but they might also be quite different. Likewise, the cultural resources and institutional supports with which each confronts their respective situation might be similar, but would more likely be dissimilar in some important ways. To put it another way, the rural Rio Grande valley borderland of Texas is not the agricultural Central Valley of California, and both differ immeasurably from the west side of Chicago. Moreover, contrasts between urban centers in the U.S. cannot be overlooked either. Los Angeles is not San Antonio; the crowded, noisy, bustling *barrio* of East L.A., where undocumented immigrants abound, stands in marked contrast to the quiet, stable west side of San Antonio. The two cities, and their Mexican American populations, have different characters, each presenting different challenges and opportunities to their inhabitants, and thus different challenges and opportunities to the Church's pastoral ministry. The NPPHM is not reflective of an investigation into these diverse social locations within the United States and their implications for the Plan's strategic goals.

The foregoing critique of the Plan's cultural lacunae does have to be mitigated to some extent by taking seriously the Plan's own call for local adaptation. [#27-8] Diocesan and parish planning efforts should afford opportunities for many of the discrete characteristics of local contexts, including those not mentioned in the Plan, to be discovered, considered and incorporated. Failure to draft local plans informed by the national document not only contravenes the NPPHM's express directive, but aborts the overall process the document seeks to advance. The NPPHM may be faulted for failing to give clearer guidance to these local efforts, and its omission of some factors which cross diocesan boundaries is not easily excused. It might have gone much further than it did in supplying local planners with the kind of critical social analysis that helps them to situate local efforts within a larger picture. However, despite these limitations, there are indications that where such diocesan and parish plans have been undertaken, the NPPHM has been found to be very useful.

Step #3: Emergence of Themes

Schreiter's third step asks for the identification of themes which emerge from the opening of culture. With regard to the Mexican American community and the NPPHM, a plurality of answers to this question might be given. However, three overlapping themes emerged clearly from our earlier study of Mexican American culture: identity, liberation and welcome.

Identity

The first two themes arise from the vicissitudes of Mexican American history, and they are closely related. We have already traced in some detail the Mexican American quest for identity, especially through the writings of Virgilio Elizondo. Mexican Americans have been ignored, their very existence overlooked by the larger cultures on both sides of the Rio Grande. Today when Mexican Americans speak of themselves as *la raza*, they disclose a long and painful process of coming to self-consciousness about their identity and place in the world. Elizondo even describes this as the birth of a people. He speaks eloquently for the Mexican Americans' desire to know who they are, where they came from, and how to tell their story theologically.

As we saw, Elizondo approaches this challenge by tracing Mexican American lineage through what he calls a "double *mestizaje*,"[11] the marriage of aboriginal peoples with Spaniards to form the Mexican identity, followed by the marriage of Mexico and the Anglo-Americans in the Southwest United States. For Elizondo this is a story of creation, a graced history to be celebrated, an unfinished narrative of intermarriage and divine adoption. It supplies Mexican Americans with a sorely lacking sense of pride, ethnic solidarity and hope for the future.

One does not have to look far in the NPPHM to hear the echoes of this brilliantly successful search to locate and describe a place in the created order. Hispanics' "language, culture, values, and traditions" are explicitly and heartily affirmed.[12] Even the language of *mestizaje* is employed in an attempt to define who these Hispanic people of today are. [#7-8] From start to finish the NPPHM seeks to promote and enhance authentic cultural identity. Its only apparent limitation in this regard is the overly generalized nature of the term *Hispanic*, as we have seen. Mexican Americans and other groups beneath this umbrella term will have to take the document as a charter for pursuing the identity peculiar to them.

Liberation

The theme of liberation comes to the fore specifically as a response to that dimension of the history of the Mexican American people characterized by conquest, subjugation and discrimination. That history issues in a present reality marked by struggle to overcome continued poverty and marginalization. Plainly, any theology suited to the Mexican American context will have to be, in some measure, a liberation theology. Similarly, any pastoral praxis which is authentically inculturated for the Mexican American people must be a liberatory praxis. Both Deck and Elizondo insist on this, as we have seen.

Thus, with regard to the theme of liberation, the question for our consideration becomes: does the NPPHM represent, aim at, engender a pastoral praxis of liberation? Our reply will have to be nuanced. On the one hand, to a great extent this question can be answered affirmatively. The NPPHM does evince a concern for the total welfare of the Hispanic people, albeit without ever resorting to the language of liberation. As we have seen, both the Plan and the Encuentro process were grounded in the social reality. Overt concern for social justice can be identified in at least thirteen sections of the document.[13] The social ministries of the Church are specifically affirmed and encouragement is given to growth in social consciousness. Moreover, the Plan even identifies the Hispanic people as themselves "a prophetic presence in the face of the materialism and individualism of [American] society." [#12]

---

11. *Galilean Journey*, pp. 9-18 and elsewhere.
12. NPPHM #4; cf. also #17 and elsewhere.
13. NPPHM #13-14, 34, 50-58, 84.

At the same time, however, we may question whether the NPPHM goes far enough in its commitment to the liberation of Hispanics, including Mexican Americans. We have already seen how the document's reading of history is quite selective. We have also seen how its assessment of the social reality is too brief, incomplete and unsystematic. While the NPPHM does contain important affirmation for liberation efforts, it falls short of an all-out effort by the Church to help the Mexican American people surmount a history of social bias and a present reality of denied access to full participation in U.S. society.

Concern for identity and concern for liberation are both essential ingredients in contextual theology. However, these two preoccupations may also be in competition with one another and perhaps even conflict. One can see the sometimes uneasy alliance of identity and liberation perspectives in the NPPHM. At many points of the document the bishops' concern to conserve the cultural heritage of Hispanics outweighs their concern for liberation. Calls for safeguarding the Catholicity of Hispanics against the incursions of fundamentalist sects, for example, are given more often and more strenuously than calls to reform unjust social structures, though the latter are present as well. One sometimes detects in the Plan some defensiveness about Hispanic identity. Interestingly, this was not generally the posture of the Third Encuentro. The Encuentro document conveys a more robust sense of pride and confidence in identity, and an eagerness to build a future even freer of constraints. The difference in tone is subtle, but noticeable.

In terms of Schreiter's two basic models of contextual theologies,[14] we may conclude that the NPPHM tends more toward the ethnographic than the liberation approach, and that it sacrifices something of the latter to the former. This is consistent with a critique made by Allan Deck of the U.S. approach to pastoral planning efforts. Deck notes that U.S. pastoral planning generally has a different intentionality and philosophical foundation than its Latin American counterparts. He says:

> Pastoral planning in the U.S. context reflects the prevailing milieu, stresses continuity, and tends to become an exercise in efficiency, in making affairs run more smoothly. Thus it becomes an instrument in promoting the modern, progressive agenda of personal freedom and well-being. But pastoral planning in the Hispanic context more appropriately ought to deal with the "material factors of domination" that are grasped principally through structural analysis. Pastoral planning, therefore, in the context of U.S. Hispanics and other marginated groups properly promotes a critique of the status quo and stresses evangelization as struggle for socioeconomic and political change.[15]

---

14. *Constructing Local Theologies*, pp. 12-5.
15. *The Second Wave*, pp. 151f.

The author goes on to note that at the CELAM conference in Puebla the themes of "communion," "participation" and "liberation" emerged. He argues that while "'communion' and 'participation' will appear to provide a more immediately relevant framework for pursuing pastoral planning," this could have the unfortunate result of relegating "liberation" to "third place."[16] Something like this appears to have happened in the formulation of the NPPHM. Communion and participation are appealed to frequently in the Plan. The social justice concern is present also, but it is in partial eclipse.

Welcome

The theme of welcome emerged primarily in regards to Mexican Americans' place within the Church itself. We saw earlier that the Catholic Church in the United States is guilty of a long history of discrimination and neglect with regard to its Mexican American members. Mexican Americans, consequently, have not felt their Church to be a welcoming faith home. In spite of the fact that the NPPHM is not completely forthright about this historical reality, it does represent a major advance on the score of making the Church more hospitable to Latinos. The mass participation in the Second and Third Encuentros under official sponsorship by the hierarchy, and the very existence of a plan which demonstrates that their efforts in the Encuentro process paid off, are profoundly important signs to many Mexican Americans that they have finally come of age in the U.S. Catholic Church. In nearly every section the Plan itself sounds the theme of welcome to a participative, pluricultural ecclesial communion. It promises this, for example, through promotion of SECs and through "creating a welcoming and inclusive atmosphere that is culturally sensitive to the marginalized" in its parishes. [#45] In addition, the Plan promises massive Church outreach to the alienated and the marginated. [#37-66]

All of the interviews I conducted with Hispanic leaders and all of the written sources I consulted are marked by hope for Mexican Americans' future within the Church. There is wide agreement that the Catholic Church in the U.S. has made real strides in the direction of embracing and valuing its Mexican American and other Hispanic members. Nearly always this hope is explicitly based on the above-mentioned series of events.

At the same time, there is also widespread agreement that much remains to be done. The general consensus seems to be that the implementation of the Plan,

---

16. *The Second Wave*, p. 152.

which would be the most potent sign of welcome of all, has been lagging.[17] Many pastoral agents feel that a more constrictive ecclesiastical climate has been taking hold. Worries are expressed that the NPPHM might even be relegated to the status of a handsome but non-functional showpiece. The last decade has seen a levelling off of Hispanic appointments to the hierarchy, together with increased Roman preoccupation with doctrinal orthodoxy and centralized discipline. Put these factors together with the contraction of financial resources facing the U.S. Church, and new pastoral initiatives are rare. Allan Deck is the most critical voice in this regard. Deck has been especially disparaging of the lack of funding for implementation of the Plan.[18] Some of the other issues raised most vehemently at the Second and Third Encuentros with regard to Hispanic participation in the Church, such as the shortage of Hispanic clergy, have not won the attention of the bishops, by and large. All in all, the outlook is cloudy for continued progress toward a church more welcoming of Mexican Americans.

Steps #4 and 5: Opening Church Tradition

The next three movements of Schreiter's map shift us from the "Culture" side of the contextual dialogue to the side of "Church Tradition." Step Four prescribes "The Opening of Church Tradition through Analysis." Like its counterpart Step One, the opening of culture through analysis, this step demands critical reflection. In the ideal, it utilizes critical "theory of the role of tradition in communities."[19] Step Four is closely allied with Step Five, "The Christian Tradition Seen as a Series of Local Theologies." In Schreiter's idealized "map" of contextual theology, the fifth step functions as a kind of hermeneutic through which the fourth step operates. That is to say, when one analyzes the tradition one does not see it as monolithic and static, but as comprised of various pieces each of which has to be contextualized in a local, historical situation in order to be understood.

Thus, Steps Four and Five invite us to examine these questions: how does church tradition function in the NPPHM? How is the Plan informed by, and normed by, church tradition that is always historically conditioned by the context(s) of its formation? In approaching these questions, it will not surprise us to find that the NPPHM is not entirely explicit about its theological perspective or assumptions. Moreover, some of the evidence will suggest that conflicting theological assumptions can be discerned within the document. The NPPHM is the result of

---

17. The possible exception here is the southeastern region, where the efforts of Fr. Mario Vizcaino, director of the South East Pastoral Institute of Miami, are widely acclaimed. Vizcaino and S.E.P.I. have made outstanding contributions in assisting dioceses in the southeast U.S. region to implement the NPPHM. Vizcaino himself told me that 22 of the 26 dioceses in this eight-state region have promulgated their own diocesan Hispanic pastoral plans based on the NPPHM. (Interview with the author, 3 Jan. 1996.)

18. Deck, "Proselytism and Hispanic Catholics: How Long Can We Cry Wolf?"

19. *Constructing Local Theologies*, p. 32.

masterful compromise, but it is not perfectly coherent in the way it understands or utilizes Christian tradition.

We turn, then, to an examination of the theological substrata of the NPPHM. The prefatory paragraphs set the document in the context of a "spirit of faith" in God, in the whole "People of God," and in Hispanic Catholics. [#2]   The understanding of faith, and of divine action, is inseparable from the church. But the employment of a familiar image from *Gaudium et Spes* is not by chance. "People of God" sets a tone and establishes a connection with Vatican II. It suggests an understanding of church that is personal, participative and communitarian.

The document's understanding of church is also warmly embracing of cultural pluralism. The bishops cite themselves in referring to the Hispanic community in the U.S. as "a blessing from God."[20] Although the document is addressed to the pastoral needs of Hispanics, "it challenges all Catholics as members of the Body of Christ." [#1]   Unfortunately, the nature of this challenge to non-Hispanic U.S. Catholics is never spelled out. But the intent seems to be to set an ecclesiological context in which diverse cultural interests coexist. This is strengthened in a subsequent introductory section, in which the bishops state that their aim is the "integration" of Hispanics in all church institutions. Their hope is for "mutual enrichment through interaction among all our cultures." [#4]

The ecclesiology expressed in the document is also strongly collaborative. The bishops emphatically affirm the *pastoral de conjunto*, which they call "not only a methodology, but an expression of the essence and mission of the Church, which is communion." [#6]   Unfortunately, again, this pregnant statement is not elaborated; we do not know precisely what the bishops had in mind in their choice of "communion" as the preeminent terminology for the church's "essence" and "mission." We do know that it was deliberate, for the "communion" theme is reiterated at least twice more. [#20, 21]   In addition, the eighteen sections which deal with *pastoral de conjunto* demonstrate that this communion ecclesiology has real substance. [#19-36] Frankly admitting that "the Hispanic Catholic experiences a lack of unity and communion in the Church's pastoral ministry," the bishops state that "the challenge here is for the laity, religious, and clergy to work together." [#19] Subsequent sections strongly promote a participative, coordinated style of ministry at all levels of the Church, from the hierarchy to the grass roots. And, in doing so, the text is remarkably devoid of cautionary reminders about episcopal or clerical prerogatives.

The "Doctrinal Framework," another of the introductory sections preceding the actual proposals, adds several more elements to the theological mix. The bishops take a sharply critical stance with regard to the larger culture of U.S. society when they begin by asserting: "The Catholic heritage and cultural identity

20. NPPHM #2; citing the 1983 pastoral letter, *The Hispanic Presence*, op. cit.

of Hispanics are threatened by the prevailing secular values of the American society." [#12] They view the Hispanic people as a "prophetic presence" standing over against those non-Gospel values. [#12] As such, Hispanics are an ally of the "prophetic" Church, which "continues to make an option for the poor and the marginalized." [#14]

The larger context here is the Church's *kerygma*:

> The mission of the Church is the continuation of Jesus' work: to announce the Kingdom of God and the means for entering it. It is the proclamation of what is to come and also an anticipation of that plenitude here and now in the process of history. The Kingdom which Jesus proclaims and initiates is so important that, in relation to it, all else is relative. [#13]

Proclamation necessitates the Church's incarnation in the multiplicity of human contexts:

> The Church, as community, carries out the work of Jesus by entering into the cultural, religious, and social reality of the people, becoming incarnate in and with the people, "in virtue of her mission and nature she is bound to no particular form of human culture, nor to any political, economic, or social system." Therefore, she is able to preach the need for conversion of everyone, to affirm the dignity of the human person, and to seek ways to eradicate personal sin, oppressive structures, and forms of injustice.[21]

Moreover, the Church "identifies with the risen Christ," whose announcement of the Kingdom "implies a new social order" and "a new style of Church as leaven." [#14] Finally, the Church is seen as the community of "the indwelling Spirit of Christ." That Spirit is the source of the Church's "solidarity," its "prophetic commitment to justice and love," and the "coresponsibility" shared by "the People of God: the Pope and the bishops, priests, religious, and laity" in the work of Jesus. [#15]

What are we to make of these various elements? In broad terms the theological approach is certainly consonant with the Third Encuentro and with all the leading Hispanic voices examined in preceding chapters. However, closer scrutiny reveals that the theology expressed in the NPPHM has a staccato quality. Discrete perspectives are expressed in compressed fashion and juxtaposed with one another with little attempt at integration. The result is, at best, only a rough harmony of overall theological perspective.

To be sure, there are some genuinely positive elements in this theological picture. For one thing, we must conclude that the NPPHM is a genuinely

---

21. NPPHM #13; the quotation is from *Gaudium et Spes*, #42.

theological enterprise. Whatever complaints one may have about the shortcomings of its theological methodology, as we shall see below, the Plan does take Christian tradition seriously as a source for human life in the Hispanic cultural context. It engages the tradition both as positive source of Hispanic Christian identity and, to a real though lesser extent, as source of challenge, redemption, liberation. The NPPHM stands squarely within the church's pastoral theological tradition, informed both by the tradition of faith and by the context it addresses.

Perhaps the strongest and most coherent dimension of the NPPHM's theology turns out to be its advancement of an ecclesiology of communion. This is a remarkable feature of the Plan and one that stands in striking contrast to what one finds in most other Roman Catholic ecclesiastical documents. We have already lamented the fact that the bishops never define what they mean by "communion." But some of its features can be deduced from various points in the document. As we have seen, *pastoral de conjunto* is one of the cornerstones of the document's ecclesiological perspective. This means that roles are differentiated, but there is remarkably little emphasis in the NPPHM upon authority or law. In the bishops' usage of the term, an ecclesiology of communion connotes collaboration, teamwork, communication among pastoral agents, planning and evaluation. This perspective assumes that all voices need to be heard and that everyone plays a part in the common mission. Moreover, it is an ecclesiology that is respectful of culture. It not only respects Hispanic culture, but even reaches toward a broader vision of a multicultural ecclesial communion in which cultures enrich, mutually support and reciprocally challenge one another. The NPPHM's portrait of the unity of the church – always a theme so central to Catholic ecclesiology – is seamlessly linked to an embrace of diversity.

The theological grounding of the NPPHM also has a decidedly contemporary caste in at least four other respects worth mentioning. First, it demonstrates an acquaintance with modern biblical scholarship, especially in the way it identifies the "Kingdom of God" as the most central theme in its understanding of the life and mission of Jesus. It places the divine reign, and not the church nor the Bible, as the point of reference for all pastoral activity. Moreover, that reign is understood to be both "not yet" and "already," both beyond human grasp and history, and at the same time breaking into human experience in the present. So the reign is not solely reserved to a future eschaton, but has meaningful implications for the present world, including the social order.

Secondly, the NPPHM is also quite contemporary theologically in its social doctrine. It presumes the tradition of Catholic social teaching. As we saw in an earlier chapter, that body of teaching has evolved dramatically in this century, especially since the Second Vatican Council. The advances in biblical scholarship mentioned in the previous paragraph have contributed to that evolution significantly. Catholic social teaching continues to develop, particularly under the influence of political and liberation theologies. Undertones of liberation theology are not difficult to discern in the document. When the bishops embrace the "option for the poor and the marginalized" [#14], for example, they are following the bishops of Latin America, who were so profoundly influenced by the theology of liberation at their Medellín and Puebla conferences. In short, the targeting of a particular disadvantaged group as the beneficiary of special material and pastoral attention can be attributed both to the official social teaching of the Catholic Church and to the social concern marking so much of the wider discourse of contemporary theology.

Thirdly, the document attends to the Third Person of the Trinity. In the Spirit the bishops find the ground of the Church's unity, the plurality of gifts in all the members, the shared responsibility for the mission and the empowerment for service to, and solidarity with, the poor and marginalized. Historically Roman Catholic theology has often tended to locate the Spirit almost exclusively within the hierarchy and the sacraments. But such is not the case with the NPPHM. Though still too brief on this point, the Plan clearly recognizes that the Spirit's activity fills the entire church.

Fourth, and closely related to the third, is the document's recognition of spirituality. Both Spirit and spirituality are themes that are finding their way into current theological scholarship with increasing frequency. Although we have seen that the NPPHM's treatment of spirituality is still somewhat awkward and structurally marginal to the main body of the document, its presence is nonetheless important and it is remarkably contemporary. Recall, for example, how the document defines spirituality: "the way of life of a people, a movement by the Spirit of God, and the grounding of one's identity as a Christian in every circumstance of life." [#16] This is not far from the approach of one eminent contemporary scholar in the field, Walter Principe. Principe gives spirituality this definition at the existential level for Christians: "Spirituality is life in the Spirit as brothers and sisters of Jesus Christ and daughters and sons of the Father."[22] On a more general level, Principe describes spirituality as

> ...the way in which a person understands and lives within his or her religion, philosophy or ethic that is viewed as the loftiest, the noblest, the most calculated to lead to the fullness of the ideal or perfection being sought.[23]

---

22. "Toward Defining Spirituality," *Sciences Religieuses/Studies in Religion* 12:2 (Spring 1983) 135.

23. "Toward Defining Spirituality," 136. See also the definitions offered by Sandra Schneiders, "Theology and Spirituality: Strangers, Rivals, or Partners?" *Horizons* 13:2 (1986) 264-7; also, Schneiders, "Spirituality in the Academy," *Theological Studies* 50 (1989) 676-97.

Additionally, the Plan evinces a quite contemporary sensitivity to the ways in which history and culture shape people's lived spirituality. This theme has been coming to the fore more and more in scholarly circles, both in the current interest in popular religion and elsewhere.[24] The Plan respects the practices of Hispanic popular piety, though not uncritically, and it fully embraces plurality of expression in the realm of spirituality. It may not carry this historical and cultural sensitivity to its logical, hermeneutical conclusion, but its incorporation into the document is an extraordinary achievement.

There are, to be sure, some serious inadequacies in the NPPHM with regard to what Schreiter demands in Steps Four and Five. We have already mentioned the lack of coherence and integration in the theological perspective. To this we can add the observation that at times the theology of the NPPHM is proposed in a top-down, deductive manner. Its doctrinal foundations are asserted rather baldly, without reference either to the context or to any process by which these particular convictions entered into the reflection on ministry in the Hispanic context. One of the assumptions guiding the theology of inculturation is that theology must be self-conscious of its own dependence upon culture, i.e., of the fact that faith requires culture for expression and actualization. The doctrinal assertions of the NPPHM, whatever their considerable merits, do not betray a satisfactory sensitivity to the fact of their own historico-cultural conditioning. Put another way, there is too little in the way of connecting material here. It may seem obvious enough, for example, why an ecclesiology of communion or the preferential option for the poor are relevant to the needs of Hispanics at this point in time, and certainly both are to be listed among the document's strengths. But there is scant articulation of the rationale for this relevance. By way of contrast, the theological approach Schreiter recommends has a more inductive method. It demands a conscious and explicit searching of the tradition for themes and convictions that are relevant to a given context.

However, this is not to say that the document does not rest upon such a process of searching the tradition. When one studies the Plan by also examining the document of the Third Encuentro, it becomes clear, at least implicitly, why certain theological themes emerged. The NPPHM would be a stronger document if it more explicitly articulated how it represents the fruit of an extended process of theological reflection on reality. To press this point further, we can recall how earlier we saw that the NPPHM does not forthrightly confront the Church's own history of discrimination and neglect with regard to Hispanics. One result of this oversight is that the document does not name and repudiate the inadequacies of the previous theologies which used to govern the Hispanic community. The Third

---

24. See, e.g., the important work by Philip Sheldrake, *Spirituality and History: Questions of Interpretation and Method* (N.Y.: Crossroad, 1992).

Encuentro, like the First and Second Encuentros before it, did exactly that. The bluntly stated historical grievance aired by the Encuentro delegates was laundered out of the final document.

Indeed the NPPHM does not evince a really consistent awareness of the local nature of theology, even though the Plan's very existence is predicated on that fact. The "Catholic heritage" of Hispanics which the bishops see as "threatened" [#12] is viewed univocally, even monolithically, at least in the formal doctrinal segment. Similarly, when the bishops speak of the church and the church's mission, they almost always mean the universal, Roman Catholic Church. Mention of the local church is hard to find, and even when present, the sense in which it is used is mainly derivative of the larger ecclesiology.

In short, if we consider the NPPHM on its own face, we would have to judge that it largely fails the test of Schreiter's fifth step. That is to say, it does not explicitly and critically view the Christian tradition as a series of local theologies. However, we need to once again place the Plan in the context of the total process, and doing so mitigates this negative judgment somewhat. If we view the NPPHM as a logical, though flawed, outgrowth of the Encuentro process, we can judge that the Plan does to some extent rest upon the implicit conviction that previous theologies need to be subjected to a hermeneutics of suspicion based on contextual factors. In the documents of the Encuentros we can see something of this critical rethinking at work. Thus, while the final language of the NPPHM itself leans in a deductive direction, we can have some confidence that it was the fruit of a more bidirectional process of dialogue with Christian tradition.

Another weakness of the NPPHM is that it is not guided by a clearly articulated theology of inculturation. The document would be greatly strengthened methodologically by more explicitness in this area. Instead, one is left to infer the document's theological underpinnings with regard to the faith-culture dynamic. The terms *inculturation* and *contextualization* are never used, though, as we have already seen, many fragments of their meaning are surely present. An oblique reference to the challenge of inculturation occurs when the bishops observe that the church's task is "to enter into the cultural, religious, and social reality of the people, becoming incarnate in and with the people." [#13] While the incarnation image as a model for inculturation has some obvious strengths, it ultimately must be rejected as too one-sided, not fully mutual, reciprocal, or dialogical.[25] The incarnation metaphor underlies the understanding of the faith and culture dynamic actually operating throughout the document. Thus, the dialogue is somewhat one-sided in favor of the church, rather than fully reciprocal and dialogical. There are, for instance, no commitments made to ecumenical or interfaith dialogue. Indeed, the document's references to other churches leave an impression of unremitting

---

25. See Shorter, pp. 81f.

competition, even hostility. In the bishops' view, the church inserts itself into various contexts, including the Hispanic. The church is the initiator, and it bears a timeless message of truth and praxis of love. To be sure, there are allusions to what the church receives from culture in return, but culture always seems to be the junior partner. The vision is not broad enough to include the possibility that local theology in the Hispanic context can not only enrich the church but even, potentially, shape and transform the tradition.

Finally, we note again that another limitation of the document is that it is very Word-centered. Proclamation (*kerygma*) figures heavily in the understanding of the church's mission. The topics that dominate the Plan's attention – catechesis, leadership formation and evangelization – are all closely aligned with this proclamation perspective. *Diakonia* and *koinonia* are also mentioned, but in minor keys. *Leitourgia* is scarce, unless one considers the bracketing sections on spirituality in that way. Why is there so little to say about liturgy, prayer, celebration, ritual, popular religion, or art? The NPPHM does not seem to envision an inculturation that infiltrates and transforms all aspects of Hispanic life in a holistic way. Authentically inculturated pastoral praxis will encompass action, relationship and symbols that appeal to the full range of human sensibilities.

Steps #6 and 7: Cultural Themes Meet Church Tradition and Shape Local Theology

Much of what we have said in the preceding pages of this chapter already speaks to Schreiter's sixth and seventh steps. In the sixth step the themes of the local cultural situation encounter church tradition. This involves, on the part of the local church, a searching of the tradition for local theologies that "parallel the local theme or need, either in content, in context, in form, or in all three."[26] This leads to the seventh step, the impact of the tradition upon the shape of local theologies. This represents the creative moment in which the wider tradition becomes resource for the construction of new contextual theology. We consider these two steps together here because they are integrally connected. While conceptually distinct, in practice they are not easily separated.

Earlier we identified the three overarching themes arising from reflection on the Mexican American situation as identity, liberation and welcome. Actually our study recognized that Mexican Americans have been engaged in a search for what they lack in each of these areas: to discover who they are, to free themselves from a condition of marginalization and oppression, and to make their home in the faith community. We saw clearly the yen for each of these in our examination of the three Encuentros. And we have already discussed in some detail the strong and weak points of the presence of these themes in the capstone document, the NPPHM.

---

26. *Constructing Local Theologies*, p. 33.

It may suffice here to offer just a few further observations on the Mexican American community's mining of the tradition for theological resources which respond to its needs in these three areas.

The Mexican American quest for identity, liberation and welcome can be seen vividly through its preeminent spokesperson, Virgilio Elizondo. Among Elizondo's many written works, probably his *The Future Is Mestizo* and *Galilean Journey* most clearly document the encounter of this search with the faith tradition. Elizondo speaks autobiographically in the former work. He recalls, for example, the identity confusion of his growing up years in the borderlands of south Texas. As a young Mexican American Elizondo had numerous "experiences of non-being,"[27] i.e., experiences which reinforced that he was neither truly Mexican nor truly American, but lived in a twilight region between the two. This led Elizondo and others like him on a search for "roots."[28] He studied the history of his own region and people, discovering aspects that were previously unknown or suppressed. This led him, as we have already seen, to see Mexican American identity as the fruit of a double conquest and double *mestizaje*.

Turning to the tradition, then, the author began to reinterpret the Mexican American history as a narrative of divine creation. He acquired new appreciation for the profound theological affirmation of *mestizo*-ness represented by Our Lady of Guadalupe. He also gained insight into the life and mission of Jesus as the prophet from Galilee. Elizondo saw that Galilee, like the American Southwest, was an ethnic and religious borderland. Jesus' Galilean origin was despised by the cultural and religious elite in Jerusalem. Elizondo even calls Jesus "a cultural *mestizo*,"[29] and thus in his own identity a symbol of rejection by the dominant culture.

Elizondo's re-appropriation of Jesus' identity as a rejected Galilean prophet opened new doors to affirming Mexican American identity theologically. Moreover, the understanding of that identity in these terms began to assume the aspect of divine election and mission.[30] Jesus as symbol of rejection becomes source of redemption for the rejected Mexican American. An identity that formerly seemed to be a handicap and a cause of humiliation becomes the source of pride and identification with Jesus. More than that, it even positions the Mexican American people to themselves participate in the mission of Jesus by playing a prophetic historical role in bringing about a multicultural future, what the author calls "universal *mestizaje*."[31]

---

27. *The Future Is Mestizo*, p. 20.
28. *The Future Is Mestizo*, p. 38.
29. *The Future Is Mestizo*, p. 79.
30. *Galilean Journey*, pp. 94ff.
31. *The Future Is Mestizo*, p. 87.

Moreover, the Jesus that Elizondo discovered positioned himself on the side of the liberation of the poor and marginalized. The discover of identity in Jesus also addressed the search for liberation. Elizondo's christology unfolded dynamically. The Galilean Jesus became for him the source of identity and, increasingly, the spring of social critique and struggle. A similar transformation came over his view of Guadalupe; its identity-giving aspects once secured, its redemptive and liberatory power began to be unleashed.

Although certainly influenced and enriched by Latin American liberation theology, Elizondo's encounter with the tradition bore a distinctive fruit, cultivated in Mexican American experience. As the author journeyed into the tradition in search of help in understanding his people's experience, he appropriated that tradition in fresh ways. In doing so he made the church his home in a way it had not been previously. In his youthful years Elizondo had found the Catholic grammar school, the parish and later the seminary to be places of cultural alienation, even rejection. In his mature years, through both his writing and his active engagement in pastoral ministry as rector of the cathedral in San Antonio, he has played an active role in making the Church a more welcoming place for Mexican Americans, and he continues to do so.

Elizondo's journey is paradigmatic. His enduring popularity over the past three decades attests to his symbolic importance as a leader within the Mexican American community. The NPPHM bears the stamp of Elizondo's labors and the labors of others on parallel journeys as well. While it was a joint effort of U.S. Hispanics, the Plan does represent the fruit of the Mexican American search for theological resources that address the needs of the Mexican American reality. The three Encuentros and the Plan itself would not have happened if Elizondo and others had not put themselves to the task of rethinking the Hispanic situation in light of the tradition.

Of course, that is not to claim that the NPPHM gathers the good fruit of that rethinking perfectly. We have already reviewed many of the ways in which the NPPHM does, and sometimes does not, well represent the process of dialogue between Mexican American culture and church tradition. Some further illumination may be gained by examining briefly just one of the major strategies proposed by the NPPHM, namely, small ecclesial communities (SECs).

The praxis of formation of SECs originated in Latin America. The hopes of many Latin American liberation theologians have been pinned on base communities. An overall appraisal of their success is not possible, but it likely would prove mixed. They seem to have been quite successful in some contexts, especially where episcopal support has been strong, but also something less than their most ardent proponents have claimed for them. Be that as it may, the importation of this strategy into the U.S. Mexican American context raises a number of questions. Although strongly endorsed in the Second and Third Encuentros, enthusiasm for SECs is not universal. They are not a major theme in the work of Virgil Elizondo. Allan Deck concurs in the generally perceived need for "small, receptive, faith-sharing community contexts."[32] But Deck also expresses some critical reservations with regard to SECs, and his position is not unfounded. The author questions whether both the efficacy and the extent of the SECs have at times been exaggerated.[33] Deck also cites recent research which suggests that SECs are a less significant influence in Latin America than the attraction of evangelical and pentecostal Christianity.[34] SECs are perceived as politicized, according to Deck, and ordinary folk "instinctively resist moving from *symbolic* to *overt* forms of protest."[35]

The social situation of the U.S. is not that of Latin America, and the NPPHM reflects disappointingly little in the way of grappling with the particular obstacles and challenges facing the SEC strategy in the U.S. context. The question as to why this strategy fits this context is not answered directly, and the answer cannot be inferred fully. SECs are not a pastoral panacea, and grandiose claims attached to them must be subjected to rigorous scrutiny.

Still, there are reasons for the emphasis placed on SECs by the Encuentros and the NPPHM, and the reasons do go deeper than mere imitation of U.S. Hispanics' Latin American cousins. Small community settings have been a facet of the Christian movement since the first century, and they have often been associated with renewal movements. They have traditionally provided, to a greater degree than typically found in larger church structures, fora for experiences of communal prayer, formation and catechesis, intensive study of the scriptures, community identity, mutual support and intimacy, collaborative action and political resistance. While some such smaller ecclesial groups have failed outright, splintered away from the larger community, or maintained a parallel existence, others have been accepted into the mainstream of the tradition and institutionalized. Among the latter one can point to many of the varied forms of vowed religious life.

Many of these historical experiences of local communities in smaller contexts hold a quite obvious attraction for contemporary U.S. Mexican Americans. To the desire to cultivate and maintain cultural identity, SECs offer a setting in which that identity can be discovered, supported and affirmed. To a marginalized people SECs

---

32. "The Crisis of Hispanic Ministry: Multiculturalism as an Ideology," *America* 163 (July 1990) 34.

33. *The Second Wave*, pp. 71-3.

34. "Reasons for Our Hope," in Deck et al., eds., *Perspectivas* (Kansas City: Sheed & Ward, 1995), p. 134; originally published in *America* 170 (23 April 1994) 12-5. The research Deck cites is that of Jorge E. Maldonado, "Building 'Fundamentalism' From the Family in Latin America," in Martin Marty and R. Scott Appleby, eds., *Fundamentalisms and Society*, vol. 2 (Chicago: U. of Chicago Press, 1993).

35. "Reasons for Our Hope," p. 134.

offer the promise of defending boundaries too long invaded by the dominant culture and the possibility of joint action to effect change. To a relationship-oriented people who experience the larger church as cold and unwelcoming, SECs offer a sense of belonging and a setting for a very personal hospitality. If the pastoral priorities for Hispanic ministry are collaboration, evangelization and formation, as the NPPHM identified them, SECs would seem to be one reasonable, historically tested channel for efforts to those ends. Local adaptation, which the Plan itself calls for, should serve to address some of the shortcomings of the introduction of this strategy into the U.S. context. Moreover, it is important to note that the attraction of SECs for many U.S. Hispanics was not merely theoretical. By the time of the Third Encuentro SECs were blossoming in many places, prompting some of the delegates to promote this strategy based on personal experience. Further harvesting of that experience will be needed in order for the SEC strategy to succeed in its aims.

Steps #8 and 9: Impacts upon Tradition and Culture

Schreiter's final two steps complete the circle by recognizing that local theologies impact both the church tradition and the culture. Religious tradition is a dynamic, ongoing process, and its development continues by means of local theological efforts. Similarly, cultures change under the influence of various forces, including the currents of theology in religious communities situated within the cultural context. In both cases our address of these steps with regard to the impact of the NPPHM can presently be little more than impressionistic and speculative.

Opinions vary as to the impact of the NPPHM on the pastoral praxis of the U.S. Catholic Church. It is widely agreed that the Encuentro process engendered tremendous good will, hope and a sense of ownership among Hispanics, including Mexican Americans. Presently in some quarters these seem to be giving way to discouragement in the face of official sloth in implementing the Plan. One fears that the opportunity for the Plan's implementation through collaboration with those most invested in it may in some places be slipping away.[36] There is no evidence to suggest that the attrition of Hispanic Catholics to other faith communities or to secularization has been stemmed at all in the years since the Plan's promulgation. Some are convinced that the document is already passé, or soon will be, as the forces of reaction and stricter discipline tighten their grip on the Church. Many point to the history of the Church's production of documents that quickly disappear into institutional archives and library shelves, and such criticism is not entirely cynical. Such observers are apt to also point to the fact that the bishops' conference

---

36. Allan Deck fears that the Third Encuentro is being "rendered a dead letter in many places throughout the U.S. church." ["The Crisis of Hispanic Ministry," 34.]

has failed to appropriate any funding for implementation of the document.[37] They may also note sadly that no other national Encuentros similar to the Third Encuentro have been held, nor are any planned. Some have found the tenor of recent officially sponsored Hispanic gatherings (like the 1995 celebration of 50 years of Hispanic ministry in San Antonio, and the recent *Encuentro 2000* in Los Angeles) to be quite different, more clerically controlled, exhortatory and celebratory, rather than dialogical. Lay participation and serious grappling with pastoral issues at such events seem to be waning. Some simply dismiss the Plan as well-intentioned but too general to be of much real assistance to pastoral agents.

There is little doubt that the implementation of the Plan has been, at best, spotty. Even some large Hispanic dioceses like San Antonio and Los Angeles have not undertaken implementation in a concerted way. But where the next step has been taken – i.e., the formulation of a diocesan plan based on the national document – there are some encouraging signs. In those places the NPPHM appears to be fostering a positive ongoing reflection on pastoral praxis in the Hispanic context. Moreover, the Plan may be serving an important function already as a publicist for the presence of Hispanics within the Church, serving notice that multiculturalism is here to stay.

On balance, the viability of the NPPHM remains in doubt, and so the document's impact on the tradition is an open question. Some leaders seem to be demonstrating that implementation can be done and that it pays off handsomely. But too often the will to do so seems to be lacking.

If it is difficult to evaluate the Plan's impact on the church and its tradition, it is even more difficult to project how the Plan may impact the cultural situation of Mexican Americans in the United States. That may well depend in large measure on the degree to which the Plan is implemented and its efficacy in achieving its pastoral goals. There is, again, little reason to believe that the social, economic, or cultural situation of the average Mexican American has been affected yet in any significant way by the commitments of the NPPHM. Perhaps in some small way the NPPHM has contributed something to the cultural self-respect of Mexican Americans and to their determination to maintain their identity and overcome the discrimination they face. The Plan certainly encourages resistance to assimilation. Perhaps, too, in some small way it serves notice that cultural diversity will be a permanent feature of U.S. society. One hopes that the NPPHM may yet have such a positive influence on the culture.

---

37. As Allan Deck observes drily, "Funds to implement the much-touted *National Pastoral Plan for Hispanic Ministry* were never allocated by the U.S. bishops." ["The Crisis of Hispanic Ministry," 34.]

Recapitulation: The Five Criteria for Local Theology

Finally, we summarize our conclusions of this chapter by turning briefly to the five criteria Schreiter suggests for evaluating local theologies.[38]   Schreiter emphasizes that these work in consort, and that a given local theology must pass all five tests to be judged positively as an authentic local expression of Christian identity.

The first criterion is cohesiveness within the tradition. Our judgment has been that the NPPHM manifests only a rough internal theological coherence. The document is wanting in terms of making explicit its theological method and in its integration of theological commitments. Despite these real limitations, it was also our judgment that the document is situated well within the bounds of the tradition. It is motivated and guided by a reading of the Gospel that is at once anchored in the tradition and yet contemporary. The NPPHM passes the test of cohesiveness.

Criterion two is the rule of belief following the rule of worship. We concluded that a weakness of the Plan is its lack of reference to worship, prayer, popular devotion and other aspects of cultural life, giving the document an imbalance in the direction of proclamation and verbosity. Despite these conclusions, however, it is clear that the NPPHM emerged from authentic spirituality within the Hispanic communities. Clearly the Encuentros were, among other things, great events of prayer. The major themes we identified – identity, liberation and welcome – are patently themes that have been brought to a prayerful encounter with the tradition. Moreover, some of the strategies of the Plan are clearly intended to facilitate prayer and root themselves in the worshipping community. SECs are perhaps the most obvious example of this. To say that the law of prayer is leading the law of belief in the Plan is perhaps overreaching. But we have identified an openness to spirituality and, at least, a relationship of mutual enrichment between the two operating in the document. We conclude, cautiously, that the NPPHM is not at odds with *lex orandi, lex credendi*.

The third criterion is judgment of the praxis generated by the local theology. We have already stated that this question cannot be definitively answered without more information from the field. We have also admitted that, unfortunately, it is possible that the Plan will remain words on a page, not translated into action. We have scrutinized the document carefully and concluded that the praxis it commends is stronger in affirming identity than it is in producing liberation, insofar as those two poles can be separated. But we have also concluded that a Christian community guided by the document in its praxis would definitely be a liberating community for Mexican Americans. While imperfect, the NPPHM represents a positive expression of the liberating praxis we find in the Gospel.

---

38. *Constructing Local Theologies*, pp. 117-21.

The fourth criterion asks for the judgment of other local churches. Although a complete answer to this question is not possible either, we can note several factors in the NPPHM's favor. We have seen that the NPPHM was born through a process that was open to the theological contributions of other local churches, especially Latin America. Some representatives of those churches – e.g., Edgard Beltrán, José Marins – even participated in the process in advisory capacities. In addition, we saw as one of the document's strengths its ecclesiology, a view of church that is respectful of cultural diversity. Finally, we note that the NPPHM was supported by Roman authorities, who bear the ministry of unity in a special way, and was endorsed by the U.S. hierarchy, the official representatives of other local churches in the Roman Catholic communion. All of these factors support the conviction that the NPPHM is being judged positively by other local churches, and thus we render a provisional positive judgment on this criterion.

Similarly, no more than a provisional answer can be given in reply to the fifth criterion, the challenge to other local churches. The Mexican American church has not generally been a missionary community. Its history of marginalization and uncertainty about its own identity have militated against that. But perhaps that is changing. In their 1983 pastoral letter the U.S. bishops affirmed the presence of the Hispanic people and urged them to raise their voices. Through the Encuentro process the prophetic voices of Mexican Americans and others were indeed heard by the rest of the church. The NPPHM continued this line by affirming that Hispanics are a "prophetic presence" within U.S. society. [#12] In short, the process of which the NPPHM is the culmination represents a new stage of development in Hispanics' assertion of themselves as challenge and gift to other local churches. It is to be hoped that that process will contribute still more to the mutual enrichment of the churches in the years to come.

CONCLUSION

Theology remains an ongoing and open process. Reflection on pastoral praxis is an undertaking whose facets seem to multiply at every turn. Constructing local theology involves a dynamic which cannot hope to be exhaustive or conclusive. Nonetheless, a few concluding remarks need to be hazarded. First we glance retrospectively at a few points of the work undertaken here, and then briefly turn our gaze forward toward the future.

In many ways, the *National Pastoral Plan for Hispanic Ministry* accurately reflects the *status quaestionis* in the Roman Catholic Church with regard to the issue of faith and culture. There are strengths and weaknesses, gaps, uncertainties and yet much cause for celebration and hope. Viewed from the perspective of the past, the NPPHM represents a huge advance toward a pastoral praxis that takes culture as a serious dialogue partner. Viewed from the perspective of the current thinking on inculturation, the NPPHM falls short of the best that we might hope for from the Church's ministry.

It is well to remember at this point that the NPPHM is a clerical, hierarchical document. It was promulgated by the U.S. bishops as the ultimate and quite distinct phase of a long gestation process. Taken by themselves, the three Encuentros represent a remarkable chapter in U.S. Catholic history, a chapter that has yet to be fully chronicled. Outside of the Hispanic community the Encuentro process is practically unknown, much less appreciated for its full significance. Within the Hispanic community, as far as I have been able to ascertain, few serious complaints about the process have been registered. On the contrary, the Third Encuentro, in particular, is more often recalled wistfully as a kind of golden moment in the life of the U.S. Hispanic Catholic community.

But, beneath the surface, the relationship between the NPPHM and the Third Encuentro remains somewhat tenuous and uneasy. We may well question whether the writing of the Plan should have been as distinct from the consultation process as it was. Why did the bishops not choose simply to endorse and adopt the final document of the Third Encuentro? Authoring a separate document, no matter how well rooted in the fruits of the Encuentro, lends at least the appearance of a distrust of the laity, or of Hispanics generally, or both. To be sure, the NPPHM has many strengths, and its very existence is a remarkable achievement, a positive sign to the Hispanic community and a source of encouragement for a culturally sensitive and diverse church. But, from the point of view of the theology of inculturation proposed here, the document of the Third Encuentro could be judged somewhat more favorably than the Plan as we have it today. The NPPHM has the stamp of episcopal authority behind it, but its content is not an improvement on the Third Encuentro.

One issue this raises, of course, is the role of the episcopal ministry in the total process of formulating the Plan. It would seem that the process might have been strengthened by having the bishops more actively involved at all steps along the way. To be sure, there was a smattering of Hispanic bishops who were deeply involved in the Encuentro and/or the actual writing of the final document. But collectively the hierarchy only became an active partner in the process once the Third Encuentro was over. If the bishops had been invested personally in the process earlier on, the need for a separate document might have been obviated. The final Plan, then, would have been more surely a product of consensus among all levels of the Church. This would have had the additional advantage of strengthening solidarity between laity and leadership.

Some of the weaknesses identified here indict both the Plan and the Encuentro process. The absence of a thorough and coherent cultural analysis is the most obvious example. In particular, Hispanic popular religion and the attraction of fundamentalist and pentecostal churches are both treated with too little sophistication. We can add to this the absence of a self-critical moment with regard to Hispanic culture. While the Encuentro and the Plan rightly affirm and celebrate Hispanic identity, too little attention is paid to the culture's shadow side, i.e., the ways in which that culture needs to be challenged, purified, or liberated by the Gospel. Of course, we have seen that cultural analysis remains a pressing frontier issue for the inculturation field as a whole. But this does not entirely excuse the weakness of both the Encuentro process and the Plan in this area. Future efforts need to do better.

Implementation appears to be another weak area of the NPPHM. Although a full-scale appraisal of the current state of the Plan's implementation has not been undertaken here, we have suggested anecdotally that it is, at best, a mixed bag. This forces the question of whether the Plan itself is defective in this area. The bishops not only have yet to appropriate the financial resources appropriate to the Plan, they have never endorsed a plan or timetable for proceeding with the implementation. Putting the NPPHM into practice is left to the conscientiousness and good will of the local bishop. There is no system of accountability in place which would ensure that the Plan is implemented on the diocesan or local levels.

Questions remain too about the Plan's relationship to other segments of the U.S. Catholic communion. Although the Third Encuentro and the NPPHM lay out ambitious goals for the Hispanic community, relatively little is demanded of the rest of us. If the Plan were taken seriously and implemented vigorously, how might the rest of the U.S. Catholic Church have to change? We can only conjecture that it would entail a fairly sweeping transformation, from the parish all the way to the national level. The Plan certainly affirms that a multicultural church is the goal, and the symbolic importance of this affirmation is not to be underestimated. But the NPPHM does not expose the responsibilities which that vision would impose on the structure and life of the whole. Moreover, the Plan fails to meet the issue of power head-on. It does not take seriously enough the symbolic significance of indigenous ministry, especially at the episcopal level. As long as Hispanics continue to be grossly under-represented in the chambers of ecclesiastical authority, there will be little reason to believe that the dominant Euroamerican segments of the U.S. church will be asked to change, adjust, make room, be inconvenienced, or even enter into true and extended dialogue. To this extent, therefore, rhetoric notwithstanding, the NPPHM does not project an inculturation process which is truly reciprocal.

Can the NPPHM serve as a model for future culturally sensitive pastoral planning efforts? My answer will be cautiously and partially affirmative. I do believe the Encuentro process, in particular, despite its shortcomings, has much to teach us. Wide consultation of those who are the intended beneficiaries of the church's ministry is both theologically essential and politically wise. The history of the Encuentro demonstrates that such consultation can indeed bear much good fruit. The process could be improved, of course, as I have suggested above, e.g., with regard to cultural analysis, the participation of the hierarchy, etc. Learning from past mistakes is part of the way forward. But the strengths of the process and even of the final document are manifest. U.S. Hispanics have demonstrated that collegial decision-making can be an enterprise that is at once loyal to the tradition, respectful of the church and its official leadership and responsible to culture. This is no mean feat.

In another sense, however, it is doubtful that the NPPHM will be allowed to serve as a model for future efforts. If the Plan goes unfunded, unimplemented, ignored or circumvented, neither inculturation nor pastoral planning will be taken seriously. Both will be discredited in the eyes of the faithful and one can rightfully then expect only cynicism and disaffection. Indeed a process and plan that promise much and deliver little might be worse than no process or plan at all.

One senses that the current moment may be nearing a juncture for U.S. Hispanics. Will the road ahead lead to continued defection from the Catholic Church, continued assimilation to the dominant culture and continued frustration of Hispanic cultural aspirations? Or might it yet lead to a more hopeful future, in which Mexican Americans and other Latinos assume a place of dignity as full partners in a multicultural church and society? The answers to these questions may well be determined by whether the *National Pastoral Plan for Hispanic Ministry* turns out to be a dead end or a step in the right direction.

SOURCES

Inculturation

Arbuckle, Gerald A. *Earthing the Gospel: An Inculturation Handbook for the Pastoral Worker.* Maryknoll, N.Y.: Orbis, 1990.

Arrupe, Pedro. "To the Whole Society." *Studies in the International Apostolate of Jesuits* 7:1 (June 1978) 1-9.

_____, ed. "A Working Paper on Inculturation." *Studies in the International Apostolate of Jesuits* 7:1 (June 1978) 10-30.

Aymes, Maria de la Cruz, et al. *Effective Inculturation and Ethnic Identity.* Vol. IX, *Inculturation: Working Papers on Living Faith and Cultures*, Arij A. Roest Crollius, ed. Rome: Pontifical Gregorian University, 1987.

Aymes, Maria de la Cruz, and Maria de los Angeles Garcia. *Principles for Inculturation of the Catechism of the Catholic Church.* Washington, D.C.: United States Catholic Conference, 1994.

Azevedo, Marcello de Carvalho. *Inculturation and the Challenges of Modernity.* Vol. I, *Inculturation: Working Papers on Living Faith and Cultures*, Arij A. Roest Crollius, ed. Rome: Pontifical Gregorian University, 1982.

Bevans, Stephen B. *Models of Contextual Theology.* Maryknoll, N.Y.: Orbis, 1992.

Bosch, David J. *Transforming Mission: Paradigm Shifts in Theology of Mission.* Maryknoll, N.Y.: Orbis, 1991.

Cenkner, William, ed. *The Multicultural Church: A New Landscape in U.S. Theologies.* N.Y.: Paulist, 1996.

Charles, Pierre. "Missiologie et Acculturation." *Nouvelle Revue Théologique* 75 (1953) 15-32.

Chupungco, Anscar J. *Cultural Adaptation of the Liturgy.* N.Y.: Paulist, 1982.

_____. *Liturgical Inculturation: Sacramentals, Religiosity, and Catechesis.* Collegeville, Minn.: Liturgical Press, 1992.

_____. *Liturgies of the Future: The Process and Methods of Inculturation.* N.Y.: Paulist, 1989.

_____. "The Roman Liturgy and Inculturation." *Federation of Diocesan Liturgical Commissions Newsletter* 21:6 (Dec. 1994) 53-6.

Costa, Ruy O., ed. *One Faith, Many Cultures: Inculturation, Indigenization, and Contextualization.* Maryknoll, N.Y.: Orbis, 1988.

Cote, Richard G. *Re-Visioning Mission: The Catholic Church and Culture in Postmodern America.* N.Y.: Paulist, 1996.

Crollius, Arij A. Roest, and Théoneste Nkéramihigo. *What Is So New about Inculturation?* Vol. V, *Inculturation: Working Papers on Living Faith and Cultures*, Arij A. Roest Crollius, ed. Rome: Pontifical Gregorian University, 1984.

Crollius, Arij A. Roest, et al. *Creative Inculturation and the Unity of Faith.* Vol. VIII,
    Inculturation: Working Papers on Living Faith and Cultures, Arij A. Roest Crollius,
    ed. Rome: Pontifical Gregorian University, 1986.

Donovan, Vincent J. *Christianity Rediscovered*, 2nd ed. Maryknoll, N.Y.: Orbis, 1982.

Dumais, Marcel, et al. *Cultural Change and Liberation in a Christian Perspective.* Vol. X,
    Inculturation: Working Papers on Living Faith and Cultures, Arij A. Roest Crollius,
    ed. Rome: Pontifical Gregorian University, 1987.

Fitzpatrick, Joseph P. *One Church, Many Cultures: The Challenge of Diversity.* Kansas
    City: Sheed & Ward, 1987.

Gallagher, Michael Paul. *Clashing Symbols: An Introduction to Faith and Culture.* N.Y.:
    Paulist, 1998.

Geertz, Clifford. *The Interpretation of Cultures.* N.Y.: Basic Books, 1973.

_____. *Local Knowledge.* N.Y.: Basic Books, 1983.

Gittins, Anthony J. *Gifts and Strangers: Meeting the Challenge of Inculturation.* N.Y.:
    Paulist, 1989.

Gremillion, Joseph, ed. *The Gospel of Peace and Justice: Catholic Social Teaching since
    Pope John.* Maryknoll, N.Y.: Orbis, 1976.

Guillemette, François. "L'apparition du concept d'inculturation: Une réception de Vatican
    II." *Mission* 2:1 (1995) 53-78.

Hesselgrave, David J., and Edward Rommen. *Contextualization: Meanings, Methods, and
    Models.* Grand Rapids: Baker Book House, 1989.

International Theological Commission. "Select Themes of Ecclesiology on the Occasion
    of the Eighth Anniversary of the Closing of the Second Vatican Council (1984)." In
    Michael Sharkey, ed., *International Theological Commission: Texts and Documents,
    1969-1985.* San Francisco: Ignatius Press, 1989. Pp. 267-304; especially §IV, "The
    People of God and Inculturation," pp. 278-82; and §V, "Particular Churches and the
    Church Universal," pp. 282-6.

John Paul II, Pope. *Catechesi Tradendae: Catechesis in Our Time.* In Austin Flannery, ed.,
    Vatican Council II: More Postconciliar Documents, vol. II. Collegeville, Minn.: The
    Liturgical Press, 1982. Pp. 762-814.

_____. *Redemptoris Missio: On the Permanent Validity of the Church's Missionary
    Mandate.* Washington, D.C.: United States Catholic Conference, 1990.

_____. *Slavorum Apostoli: In Commemoration of the Eleventh Centenary of the
    Evangelizing Work of Saints Cyril and Methodius.* Boston: St. Paul Editions, 1985.

Kraft, Charles H. *Christianity in Culture: A Study in Dynamic Biblical Theologizing in
    Cross-Cultural Perspective.* Maryknoll, N.Y.: Orbis, 1979.

Lane, Dermot A. "Faith and Culture: The Challenge of Inculturation," in Dermot A. Lane,
    ed., *Religion and Culture in Dialogue: A Challenge for the Next Millenium.* Dublin:
    Columba Press, 1993. Pp. 11-39.

Luzbetak, Louis J. *The Church and Cultures: New Perspectives in Missiological
    Anthropology*, rev. ed. Maryknoll, N.Y.: Orbis, 1988.

Masson, Joseph. "L'Eglise ouverte sur le monde." *Nouvelle Revue Théologique* 84:10
    (Dec. 1962) 1032-43.

_____. "Fonction missionaire, fonction d'Eglise" (2 parts). *Nouvelle Revue Théologique* 80 (1958) 1042-61, and 81 (1959) 41-59.

_____. "La mission à la lumière de l'Incarnation." *Nouvelle Revue Théologique* 98:10 (Dec. 1976) 865-90.

Paul VI, Pope. *Evangelii Nuntiandi: On Evangelization in the Modern World.* Washington, D.C.: U.S. Catholic Conference, 1975.

_____. *Populorum Progressio: On the Development of Peoples.* In Joseph Gremillion, ed., *The Gospel of Peace and Justice: Catholic Social Teaching since Pope John.* Maryknoll, N.Y.: Orbis, 1976. Pp. 387-415.

Peelman, Achiel. *L'Inculturation: L'Eglise et les Cultures.* Paris: Desclée, 1988.

Poupard, Cardinal Paul. *L'Église au défi des cultures: Inculturation et Evangélisation.* Paris: Desclée, 1989.

Scheuer, Jacques. "Inculturation: Presentation of the Topic." *Lumen Vitae* 40:1 (1985) 10-18.

Schineller, Peter. *A Handbook on Inculturation.* N.Y.: Paulist, 1990.

_____. "Inculturation as the Pilgrimage to Catholicity." In Johann-Baptist Metz and Edward Schillebeeckx, eds., *World Catechism or Inculturation?* (*Concilium* 204). Edinburgh: T. & T. Clark Ltd., 1989. Pp. 98-106.

Schner, George P., ed. *The Church Renewed: The Documents of Vatican II Reconsidered.* Lanham, Maryland: University Press of America, 1986.

Schreiter, Robert J. "Communication and Interpretation across Cultures: Problems and Prospects." *International Review of Mission* 85:337 (1996) 227-39.

_____. *Constructing Local Theologies.* Maryknoll, N.Y.: Orbis, 1985.

_____. "Defining Sycretism: An Interim Report." *International Bulletin of Missionary Research* 17 (April 1993) 50-3.

_____. "Faith and Cultures: Challenges to a World Church." *Theological Studies* 50 (1989) 744-60.

_____. *The New Catholicity: Theology between the Global and the Local.* Maryknoll, N.Y.: Orbis, 1997.

Shorter, Aylward. *Toward a Theology of Inculturation.* Maryknoll, N.Y.: Orbis, 1988.

Standaert, Nicolas. "L'histoire d'un néologisme." *Nouvelle Revue Théologique* 110 (1988) 555-70.

Starkloff, Carl F. "Ecclesiology as Praxis: The Use of Models in Planning for Mission and Ministry." *Pastoral Sciences* 9 (1990) 175-98.

_____. "Inculturation and Cultural Systems" (2 parts). *Theological Studies* 55 (1994) 66-81 and 274-94.

_____. "Keepers of Tradition: The Symbol Power of Indigenous Ministry." *Kérygma* 23:52 (1989) 3-120.

_____. "The Problem of Syncretism in the Search for Inculturation." *Mission* 1 (1994) 75-94.

Tanner, Norman P., ed. *Decrees of the Ecumenical Councils,* vol. 2. Washington, D.C.: Georgetown University Press, 1990. Documents of the Second Vatican Council, pp. 817-1135.

Tracy, David. *The Analogical Imagination: Christian Theology and the Culture of Pluralism.* N.Y.: Crossroad, 1981.

_____. *Dialogue with the Other: The Inter-Religious Dialogue.* Grand Rapids: Wm. B. Eerdmans, 1990.

_____. *Plurality and Ambiguity: Hermeneutics, Religion, Hope.* San Francisco: Harper & Row, 1987.

Udoidem, S. Iniobong. *Pope John Paul II on Inculturation: Theory and Practice.* Lanham, Md.: University Press of America, 1996.

Villamán, Marcos J. "Church and Inculturation: Modernity and Culture in Latin America." *Journal of Hispanic/Latino Theology* 1:3 (May 1994) 5-46.

Latin America

Barreiro, Alvaro. *Basic Ecclesial Communities: The Evangelization of the Poor.* Maryknoll, N.Y.: Orbis, 1982.

Berryman, Phillip. *Liberation Theology.* N.Y.: Pantheon, 1987.

Boff, Clodovis. *Theology and Praxis: Epistemological Foundations.* Maryknoll, N.Y.: Orbis, 1987.

Boff, Leonardo. *Ecclesiogenesis: The Base Communities Reinvent the Church.* Translated by Robert R. Barr. Maryknoll, N.Y.: Orbis, 1986.

_____. *Church: Charism and Power.* Translated by John W. Diercksmeier. N.Y.: Crossroad, 1985.

_____. *Salvation and Liberation.* Maryknoll, N.Y.: Orbis, 1984.

Candelaria, Michael R. *Popular Religion and Liberation: The Dilemma of Liberation Theology.* Albany: State University of New York Press, 1990.

Conferencia General del Episcopado Latinoamericano (CELAM II: Medellín, Colombia, 1968). *The Church in the Present-Day Transformation of Latin America in the Light of the Council,* 2 vols. Bogotá: General Secretariat of CELAM, 1970-73.

Conferencia General del Episcopado Latinoamericano (CELAM III: Puebla, Mexico, 1979). *Evangelization at Present and in the Future of Latin America: Conclusions.* Washington, D.C.: National Conference of Catholic Bishops, 1979.

Conferencia General del Episcopado Latinoamericano (CELAM III: Puebla, Mexico, 1979). *Visión Pastoral de America Latina: Equipo de Reflexión, Departamentos y Secciones del CELAM.* Bogotá: Consejo Episcopal Latinoamericano, 1978.

Conferencia General del Episcopado Latinoamericano (CELAM IV: Santo Domingo, Dominican Republic, 1992). *Documento de Consulta: Nueva Evangelización, Promoción Humana.* Bogotá: Consejo Episcopal Latinoamericano, 1991.

Conferencia General del Episcopado Latinoamericano (CELAM IV: Santo Domingo, Dominican Republic, 1992). *Conclusions: New Evangelization, Human Development, Christian Culture.* Washington, D.C.: U.S. Catholic Conference, 1993.

Cook, Guillermo. *The Expectation of the Poor: Latin American Base Ecclesial Communities in Protestant Perspective.* Maryknoll, N.Y.: Orbis, 1985.

Dussel, Enrique. "Popular Religion as Oppression and Liberation: Hypotheses on Its Past and Present in Latin America." In Norbert Greinacher and Norbert Mette, eds., *Popular Religion (Concilium* 186), pp.82-94. Edinburgh: T. & T. Clark, 1986.

Eagleson, John, and Philip Scharper, eds. *Puebla and Beyond: Documentation and Commentary.* Maryknoll, N.Y.: Orbis, 1979.

Gutiérrez, Gustavo. *Las Casas: In Search of the Poor of Jesus Christ.* Translated by Robert R. Barr. Maryknoll, N.Y.: Orbis, 1993.

_____. *A Theology of Liberation,* rev. ed. Translated and edited by Sister Caridad Inda and John Eagleson. Maryknoll, N.Y.: Orbis, 1988.

_____. *We Drink from Our Own Wells.* Translated by Matthew J. O'Connell. Maryknoll, N.Y.: Orbis, 1984.

Hebblethwaite, Margaret. *Base Communities: An Introduction.* Mahwah, N.J.: Paulist, 1994.

Hennelly, Alfred T. *Theology for a Liberating Church: The New Praxis of Freedom.* Washington, D.C.: Georgetown University Press, 1989.

_____, ed. *Liberation Theology: A Documentary History.* Maryknoll, N.Y.: Orbis, 1990.

_____, ed. *Santo Domingo and Beyond: Documents and Commentaries from the Fourth General Conference of Latin American Bishops.* Maryknoll, N.Y.: Orbis, 1993.

Hewitt, W. E. *Basic Christian Communities and Social Change in Brazil.* Lincoln, Nebraska: University of Nebraska Press, 1991.

International Ecumenical Congress of Theology. *The Challenge of Basic Christian Communities.* S. Torres and J. Eagleson, eds. Trans. by John Drury. Maryknoll, N.Y.: Orbis, 1981.

Irarrázaval, Diego. "Catolicismo popular en la teología de la liberación." In V. Elizondo et al., *Teología y Liberación: Religión, Cultura y Ética.* Lima, Perú: Instituto Bartolomé de las Casas, 1991. Pp. 71-105.

Levine, Daniel H. *Popular Voices in Latin American Catholicism.* Princeton, N.J.: Princeton University Press, 1992.

Mainwaring, Scott, and Alexander Wilde, eds. *The Progressive Church in Latin America.* Notre Dame, Indiana: University of Notre Dame Press, 1989.

McGrath, Marcos. "The Impact of *Gaudium et Spes*: Medellín, Puebla, and Pastoral Creativity." In Joseph Gremillion, ed., *The Church and Culture since Vatican II: The Experience of North and Latin America.* Notre Dame, Indiana: University of Notre Dame Press, 1985. Pp. 61-73.

Pelton, Robert S. *From Power to Communion: Toward a New Way of Being Church Based on the Latin American Experience.* Notre Dame, Indiana: University of Notre Dame Press, 1994.

Richard, Pablo. *The Church Born by the Force of God in Central America.* N.Y.: Circus Publications, 1985.

Segundo, Juan Luis. *The Liberation of Theology.* Translated by John Drury. Maryknoll, N.Y.: Orbis, 1976.

Sobrino, Jon. *Spirituality of Liberation: Toward Political Holiness.* Maryknoll, N.Y.: Orbis, 1988.

_____. *The True Church and the Poor.* Maryknoll, N.Y.: Orbis, 1984.

U.S. Hispanics

Abalos, David T. *Latinos in the United States: The Sacred and the Political.* Notre Dame, Indiana: University of Notre Dame Press, 1986.

Acuña, Rodolfo. *Occupied America: A History of Chicanos,* 3rd ed. N.Y.: Harper & Row, 1988.

Aquino, María Pilar. "Directions and Foundations of Hispanic/Latino Theology: Toward a *Mestiza* Theology of Liberation." *Journal of Hispanic/Latino Theology* 1:1 (November 1993) 5-21.

Bishops' Committee for Hispanic Affairs, National Conference of Catholic Bishops. *Communion and Mission: A Guide for Bishops and Pastoral Leaders on Small Church Communities.* Washington, D.C.: United States Catholic Conference, 1995.

Bishops' Committee for Hispanic Affairs, National Conference of Catholic Bishops. *Leaven for the Kingdom of God.* Washington, D.C.: United States Catholic Conference, 1990.

Blanchard, David. "Hispanic Pastoral Life: Endorsing a Latin Style." *Church* 4:3 (Fall 1988) 22-27.

Conclusiones: Primer Encuentro Nacional Hispano de Pastoral. Washington, D.C.: United States Catholic Conference, 1972.

Davis, Kenneth. "De Encuentro a Reconocimiento: The U.S. Hispanic Church since 1987." Unpubished paper obtained from the author, photocopy [1995]. 15 pages.

_____. "The Hispanic Shift: Continuity Rather than Conversion?" *Journal of Hispanic/Latino Theology* 1:3 (May 1994) 68-79.

Deck, Allan Figueroa. "The Challenge of Evangelical/ Pentecostal Christianity to Hispanic Catholicism in the United States." Unpublished lecture given at the Cushwa Center for the Study of American Catholicism, University of Notre Dame, 1992.

_____. "The Crisis of Hispanic Ministry: Multiculturalism as an Ideology." *America* 163 (21 July 1990) 33-6.

_____. "Fundamentalism and the Hispanic Catholic." *America* 152 (26 Jan. 1985) 64-6.

_____. "Hispanic Ministry Comes of Age." *America* 154 (17 May 1986) 400-2.

_____. "Proselytism and Hispanic Catholics: How Long Can We Cry Wolf?" *America* 159 (10 Dec. 1988) 485-90.

_____. "Rising Voices in a Dialogue of and for the Americas." *America* 166 (8 Feb. 1992) 98-101.

_____. *The Second Wave.* N.Y.: Paulist, 1989.

_____. "The Trashing of the Fifth Centenary." *America* 167 (26 Dec. 1992) 499-501.

_____, ed. *Frontiers of Hispanic Theology in the United States.* Maryknoll, N.Y.: Orbis, 1992.

Deck, Allan Figueroa, Yolanda Tarango, and Timothy M. Matovina, eds. *Perspectivas: Hispanic Ministry.* Kansas City: Sheed & Ward, 1995.

Dolan, Jay P. *The American Catholic Experience: A History from Colonial Times to the Present.* Garden City, N.Y.: Image Books, 1985.

_____, ed. *The American Catholic Parish: A History from 1850 to the Present*, 2 vols. N.Y.: Paulist, 1987.

Dolan, Jay P., and Gilberto M. Hinojosa, eds. *Mexican Americans and the Catholic Church, 1900-1965.* Notre Dame, Indiana: University of Notre Dame Press, 1994.

Dolan, Jay P., and Allan Figueroa Deck, eds. *Hispanic Catholic Culture in the U.S.: Issues and Concerns.* Notre Dame, Indiana: University of Notre Dame Press, 1994.

Elizondo, Virgilio P. *Christianity and Culture: An Introduction to Pastoral Theology and Ministry for the Bicultural Community.* Huntington, Indiana: Our Sunday Visitor, 1975.

_____. *Creemos en Jesucristo: Catequesis Hispana para Adultos.* Liguori, Missouri: Liguori Publications, 1981.

_____. *The Future is Mestizo: Life Where Cultures Meet.* Oak Park, Illinois: Meyer-Stone Books, 1988.

_____. *Galilean Journey: The Mexican-American Promise.* Maryknoll, N.Y.: Orbis, 1983.

_____. "Hispanic Theology and Popular Piety: From Interreligious Encounter to a New Ecumenism." *Proceedings of the Catholic Theological Society of America* 48 (1993) 1-14.

_____. *Guadalupe: Mother of the New Creation.* Maryknoll, N.Y.: Orbis, 1997.

_____. "El mestizaje como lugar teológico." In V. Elizondo et al., *Teología y Liberación: Religión, Cultura y Ética.* Lima, Perú: Instituto Bartolomé de las Casas, 1991. Pp. 13-41.

_____. *Mestizaje: The Dialectic of Cultural Birth and the Gospel: A Study in the Intercultural Dimension of Evangelization.* San Antonio: Mexican American Cultural Center, 1978.

_____. *La Morenita: Evangelizer of the Americas.* San Antonio: Mexican American Cultural Center, 1980.

_____. "The New Humanity of the Americas." In Leonardo Boff and V. Elizondo, eds., *1492-1992: The Voice of the Victims* (*Concilium* 1990/6). Philadelphia: Trinity Press International, 1990.

_____. "Popular Religion as Support of Identity: A Pastoral-Psychological Case-Study Based on the Mexican American Experience in the USA." In Norbert Greinacher and Norbert Mette, eds., *Popular Religion* (*Concilium* 186), pp. 36-43. Edinburgh: T. & T. Clark, 1986.

_____, ed. *Way of the Cross: The Passion of Christ in the Americas.* Maryknoll, N.Y.: Orbis, 1992.

Elizondo, Virgilio P., and Angela Erevia. *Our Hispanic Pilgrimage.* San Antonio: Mexican American Cultural Center, 1980.

Espín, Orlando O. "Pentecostalism and Popular Catholicism: The Poor and *Traditio.*" *Journal of Hispanic/Latino Theology* 3:2 (Nov. 1995) 14-43.

_____. "Popular Religion as an Epistemology (of Suffering)." *Journal of Hispanic/Latino Theology* 2:2 (November 1994) 55-78.

Fernández-Shaw, Carlos. *The Hispanic Presence in North America: From 1492 to Today.* N.Y.: Facts on File, 1991.

Galerón, Soledad, Rosa Maria Icaza, and Rosendo Urrabazo, eds. *Prophetic Vision: Pastoral Reflections on the National Pastoral Plan for Hispanic Ministry.* Kansas City: Sheed & Ward, 1992.

Gann, L. H., and Peter J. Duignan. *The Hispanics in the United States: A History.* Boulder, Colorado: Westview Press, 1986.

García, Sixto J. "Sources and Loci of Hispanic Theology." *Journal of Hispanic/Latino Theology* 1:1 (November 1993) 22-43.

Gastón, María Luisa, ed. *Proceedings of the II Encuentro Nacional Hispano de Pastoral.* Washington, D.C.: Secretariat for Hispanic Affairs, National Conference of Catholic Bishops, United States Catholic Conference, 1978.

Goizueta, Roberto S. *Caminemos con Jesús: Toward a Hispanic/Latino Theology of Accompaniment.* Maryknoll, N.Y.: Orbis, 1995.

_____. "The Preferential Option for the Poor: The CELAM Documents and the NCCB Pastoral Letter on U.S. Hispanics as Sources for U.S. Hispanic Theology." *Journal of Hispanic/Latino Theology* 3:2 (November 1995) 65-77.

_____, ed. *We Are a People! Initiatives in Hispanic-American Theology.* Minneapolis: Fortress, 1992.

González, Roberto O., and Michael J. LaVelle. *The Hispanic Catholic in the United States: A Socio-Cultural and Religious Profile.* N.Y.: Northeast Catholic Pastoral Center for Hispanics, 1985.

Greeley, Andrew. "Defection among Hispanics." *America* 159:3 (30 July 1988) 61-2.

Guerrero, Andrés G. *A Chicano Theology.* Maryknoll, N.Y.: Orbis, 1987.

Hemrick, Eugene F., ed. *Strangers and Aliens No Longer: Part One: The Hispanic Presence in the Church of the United States.* Washington, D.C: United States Catholic Conference, 1993.

Hornor, Louise L., ed. *Hispanic Americans: A Statistical Sourcebook.* Palo Alto, California: Information Publications, 1995.

Isasi-Díaz, Ada María, and Fernando F. Segovia, eds. *Hispanic/Latino Theology: Challenge and Promise.* Minneapolis: Fortress Press, 1996.

Isasi-Díaz, Ada María, and Yolanda Tarango. *Hispanic Women: Prophetic Voice in the Church.* San Francisco: Harper & Row, 1988.

Kanellos, Nicolás, ed. *The Hispanic-American Almanac.* Detroit: Gale Research Inc., 1993.

Lampe, Philip E., ed. *Hispanics in the Church: Up from the Cellar.* San Francisco: Catholic Scholars Press, 1993.

Lopez, Vicente. Interview by author, 31 Oct. 1995, Notre Dame.

Mirandé, Alfredo. *The Chicano Experience: An Alternative Perspective.* Notre Dame, Indiana: University of Notre Dame Press, 1985.

Morales, Rebecca, and Frank Bonilla, eds. *Latinos in a Changing U.S. Economy.* Newbury Park, California: Sage Publications, 1993.

Mosqueda, Lawrence J. *Chicanos, Catholicism, and Political Ideology.* Lanham, Maryland: University Press of America, 1986.

National Conference of Catholic Bishops. *National Pastoral Plan for Hispanic Ministry.* Washington, D.C.: United States Catholic Conference, 1987. Originally published in *Origins* 17:26 (Dec. 10, 1987) 449-463.

National Conference of Catholic Bishops. *The Hispanic Presence: Challenge and Commitment.* Washington, D.C.: United States Catholic Conference, 1983.

Pérez, Arturo. *Popular Catholicism: A Hispanic Perspective.* Washington, D.C.: The Pastoral Press, 1988.

Pineda, Ana María, and Robert Schreiter, eds. *Dialogue Rejoined: Theology and Ministry in the United States Hispanic Reality.* Collegeville: Liturgical Press, 1995.

Ramírez, Ricardo. *Fiesta, Worship and Family.* San Antonio: Mexican American Cultural Center, 1981.

_____, ed. *Faith Expressions of Hispanics in the Southwest*, rev. ed. San Antonio: Mexican American Cultural Center, 1990.

Reddy, Marlita A., ed. *Statistical Record of Hispanic Americans.* Detroit: Gale Research Inc., 1993.

Rodriguez, Jeanette. *Our Lady of Guadalupe: Faith and Empowerment among Mexican-American Women.* Austin, Texas: University of Texas Press, 1994.

Romero, C. Gilbert. *Hispanic Devotional Piety: Tracing the Biblical Roots.* Maryknoll, N.Y.: Orbis, 1991.

Samora, Julian, and Patricia Vandel Simon. *A History of the Mexican-American People*, rev. ed. Notre Dame, Indiana: University of Notre Dame Press, 1993.

Sandoval, Moíses. *Hispanic Challenges to the Church.* Washington, D.C.: Secretariat for Hispanic Affairs, United States Catholic Conference, 1978.

_____. *On the Move: A History of the Hispanic Church in the United States.* Maryknoll, N.Y.: Orbis, 1990.

_____, ed. *Fronteras: A History of the Latin American Church in the USA since 1513.* San Antonio: Mexican American Cultural Center, 1983.

Scheuring, Thomas J. *Evangelii Nuntiandi* and the Puebla Final Document: Their Effects on the Mission of Evangelization with the Poor. N.Y.: Ph.D. thesis, Fordham University, 1990.

Schick, Frank L., and Renee Schick, eds. *Statistical Handbook on U.S. Hispanics.* Phoenix: Oryx Press, 1991.

Sedillo, Pablo, ed. *Prophetic Voices: The Document on the Process of the III Encuentro Nacional Hispano de Pastoral.* Washington, D.C.: Secretariat for Hispanic Affairs, United States Catholic Conference, 1986.

Shorris, Earl. *Latinos: A Biography of the People.* N.Y.: Avon Books, 1992.

Spicer, Edward H. *Cycles of Conquest: The Impact of Spain, Mexico, and the United States on the Indians of the Southwest, 1533-1960.* Tucson, Arizona: University of Arizona Press, 1962.

Stern, Robert L. "Evolution of Hispanic Ministry in the New York Archdiocese." In *Hispanics in New York: Religious, Cultural and Social Experiences*, vol. II. N.Y.: Office of Pastoral Research, Archdiocese of New York, 1982.

Stevens-Arroyo, Anthony M., ed. *Prophets Denied Honor: An Anthology on the Hispanic Church in the United States.* Maryknoll, N.Y.: Orbis, 1980.

Stevens-Arroyo, Anthony M., and Gilbert R. Cadena, eds. *Old Masks, New Faces: Religion and Latino Identities.* N.Y.: Bildner Center for Western Hemisphere Studies, 1995.

Tovar, Consuelo, ed. *Documento de Trabajo: III Encuentro Nacional Hispano de Pastoral, Edición Bilingüe.* Washington, D.C.: Secretariat for Hispanic Affairs, United States Catholic Conference, 1985.

Valdivieso, Rafael, and Cary Davis. *U.S. Hispanics: Challenging Issues for the 1990s.* Washington, D.C.: Population Reference Bureau, 1988.

Vilar, J. Juan Díaz. *Somos Una Sola Iglesia/We Are One Church: Ten Themes for Reflection on the U.S. Bishops' Pastoral Letter "The Hispanic Presence: Hope and Commitment."* N.Y.: Northeast Catholic Pastoral Center for Hispanics, 1984.

Villamán, Marcos J. "Church and Inculturation: Modernity and Culture in Latin America." *Journal of Hispanic/Latino Theology* 1:3 (May 1994) 5-46.

Vizcaino, Mario. Interview by author, 3 January 1996, Miami. Tape recording.

Wright, Robert E. "If It's Official, It Can't Be Popular? Reflections on Popular and Folk Religion." *Journal of Hispanic/Latino Theology* 1:3 (May 1994) 47-67.

Finito di stampare nel mese di marzo 2001

Tipografia "Giovanni Olivieri" di E. Montefoschi ~ Via dell'Archetto, 10-11-12 – 00187 Roma